# THE DRAW

# THE DRAW

## A MEMOIR

# LEE SIEGEL

FARRAR, STRAUS AND GIROUX   NEW YORK

Farrar, Straus and Giroux
18 West 18th Street, New York 10011

Library of Congress Cataloging-in-Publication Data
Names: Siegel, Lee, 1957– author.
Title: The draw : a memoir / Lee Siegel.
Description: First edition. | New York : Farrar, Straus and Giroux, 2017.
Identifiers: LCCN 2016033248 | ISBN 9780374178055 (hardback) |
    ISBN 9780374714000 (e-book)
Subjects: LCSH: Siegel, Lee, 1957– . | Authors, American—20th century—
    Biography. | Critics—United States—Biography. | Debt—United States. |
    Downward mobility (Social sciences)—United States. | Social values—
    United States. | United States—Moral conditions. | BISAC: BIOGRAPHY &
    AUTOBIOGRAPHY / Personal Memoirs.
Classification: LCC PS3619.I3785 Z46 2017 | DDC 818/.603 [B]—dc23
LC record available at https://lccn.loc.gov/2016033248

Designed by Jonathan D. Lippincott

Our books may be purchased in bulk for promotional, educational,
or business use. Please contact your local bookseller or the Macmillan Corporate
and Premium Sales Department at 1-800-221-7945, extension 5442,
or by e-mail at MacmillanSpecialMarkets@macmillan.com.

www.fsgbooks.com
www.twitter.com/fsgbooks • www.facebook.com/fsgbooks

1   3   5   7   9   10   8   6   4   2

*For my children, Julian and Harper*

And if that diamond ring turns brass,
Mama's gonna buy you a looking glass.

# Author's Note

Most names and some identifying information about people in this book have been changed.

# Contents

# THE DRAW

# 1

# HAVE MERCY

The late August night before I went away to college I stood with my grandfather on 231st Street in the Bronx. We were standing on a rise in the street, a little hill that sloped downward in either direction. I could hear the subway clatter past on the elevated tracks over Broadway, two blocks to the east.

Over my grandfather's shoulder was an incandescent coin, a full moon. What is she doing to us? he said in a choked voice. He was referring to my mother, who had decided to leave my father. Despite Menka's seventy years and his receding mane of pure white hair, he looked like a boy, standing there confused, despairing, under the full silvery moon, with his round, swarthy face and soft brown eyes, on the little hill.

I don't know, I said. I don't understand. I had always called him Papa as a child. Now that I was older I couldn't call him that. "Grandpa" was out of the question. It lacked the almost tangible warmth of the Russian words I heard my grandparents speak to each other. Walter Brennan, on one of the TV shows I watched obsessively, *The Real McCoys*, was someone I would call Grandpa. Yet I could not bring myself to call my grandfather by the names everyone else called him by: Menka, which was a Russian diminutive for Emanuel, or Manny, which he somehow acquired as the American version of the Russian diminutive. He was Papa. So for some time I hadn't called him anything at all. Instead I would smile at him, and he would smile at me. I buried my face in his chest.

Make a life for yourself, he said. *Make a life for yourself.* That was my grandfather's precious phrase. So was: *You have to have something to fall back on.* Born in Odessa, he had lost much of his family in the 1905 Odessa pogrom, when Cossacks got off their horses to stride through the seaside town and butcher Jewish men, women, and children in the street.

My grandfather, who was barely a toddler then, never talked about the pogrom. I never knew whether his parents were killed or survived or, if they did survive, what happened to them. He never spoke about his parents. Twelve years later, he said, he made his way to Moscow with two older sisters and an older brother. I had met them once or twice when I was very young: Yeva, Nova, and Zema, all of them old, kind and quiet as they caressed me with fingers that were long and old, with peels of dry, white skin that felt rough against my face.

The revolution had broken out. My grandfather covered that event with terse comedy. Someone handed him a rifle, he said. He shot a few bullets into the air. Then he made his way to a boat. There he met his sisters and brother, and all of them sailed to America.

For Jews such as my grandfather, who had suffered in Europe, history was made strictly by the goyim. Like professional sports, history was not a Jewish field. As he told the story of his escape into a new life, with its blatant omissions, exaggerations, and possibly wholesale fabrications, his face took on a glittering sardonic aspect, hard and grasping and touched with malice. You could not imagine that face wrinkling into tears unless you had worked out the equation between excessive feeling and paucity of empathy.

When my mother, his daughter, was about fifteen, she told him that she wanted to smoke. Fine, he said, handing her his cigar. Suck on this and take in as much smoke as you can. Hold it in for as long as you can without breathing. She followed his instructions and vomited until she had nothing left to vomit. That is how you smoke, he said, laughing. Upon learning from my younger brother, who was then about eight, that he was afraid of going down alone to the basement of my grandparents' apartment building, where there was a vending machine that dispensed milk, my grandfather took my brother by the hand, walked him into the hallway, and rang for the elevator. When it arrived, he gently guided my brother into it. Handing him a quarter for the machine, he pressed the button for the basement and, smiling, waved goodbye to my terrified brother as the elevator doors closed.


Living with relatives in the Bronx, Menka worked at various jobs until, as a young man, he found a position as a bellboy at the President Hotel on West Forty-eighth Street in Times Square. He stayed there for decades. Whereas he was reticent about Odessa, he enjoyed telling stories about his experiences at the President, a tony hotel much beloved by Harlem's artistic elite. The fact of my grandfather working as a bellboy, not for rich white people but for rich black people, made a lasting impression on me. The black porters at Grand Central Station, whom I sometimes saw as a young boy on visits to New York City with my family, and on our occasional family trip by rail, mingled in my imagination with my grandfather.

I saw these black men through the eyes of a boy, fifty years ago, so you must forgive a description that now seems insensitive.

But, fifty years ago, I thought I saw that within the yoke of their menial work they moved inside their own free space. I cherished this dignity-in-harness that I also thought I found in Menka, who carried other people's things for a living.

The President Hotel was the site of a famous nightclub, Adrian's Tap Room. Fats Waller and other prominent jazz musicians of the day liked to perform there. Harry Belafonte once gave my grandfather a radio as a gift, Menka told us, his face radiant with pride. Diana Ross presented him with a fifty-dollar tip. His round, boyish face suddenly gleaming and sardonic, he would tell us about the treasures he found left behind in the hotel and kept: jewelry, watches, clothes, money. He never questioned the rightness of making off with these things. They were the spoils of a vicious world.

Rose, my grandmother and Menka's wife, was born in Minsk. She emigrated to America with her parents in the 1920s. Her four older sisters remained in Minsk and were shot with their husbands and children in a mass grave by the SS after the Nazis invaded the Soviet Union.

Menka won Rose's heart with a trick that he performed with money. Every day he would come into her parents' candy store in the Bronx, where Rose worked behind the counter. He would produce a dollar bill from his pocket. Holding it up for her to see, he made it disappear. Then he produced it again. That was how Menka thought of money. It was the foundation of love, life, and happiness but also an object of contempt because, like a prostitute, it bestowed itself without discrimination.

The other side of Menka's idea of money as something like snow, there for the taking, was his fear that once he possessed it, the money would vanish. At the end of his life, he and Rose lived comfortably in their aging, medium-rise apartment building on 231st Street, half a block from where I said goodbye to him that August night. They stayed afloat because their rent was protected by the city, and by means of Menka's modest savings.

Nevertheless, as he and Rose sat in the back of a taxi that was rushing them to a hospital after Menka suffered a heart attack—the ambulance they called for was taking too long—he whispered to Rose, There's forty dollars taped underneath the medicine cabinet. Then he died.

As a young girl, Lola, my mother, aspired to be an actress. At the age of seventeen, just after graduating from high school, she auditioned at the Actors Studio, even then a legendary place, and got accepted. She found herself in a class with Marlon Brando, who was either a student in the class or a visitor, I was never sure.

Brando, according to my mother, always came to class wearing old, dirty clothes that recalled the torn, sweaty T-shirt that he had made famous in *A Streetcar Named Desire*. One day, on a dare from some of the other young women in the class, my mother went up to Brando and asked him why he did not come to class wearing nicer clothes. "Fuck you," Brando said.

My mother told this story over and over again. Until her separation from my father, she never used the word "fuck." She said "Eff you." When she said it, her eyes shone with a faraway look. You would have thought Brando had said "I love you." My mother, like Menka, had a tremendous capacity for absorbing humiliation.

After taking a few classes at the Actors Studio, she declared to Menka that she wanted to be an actress and a singer. He slapped her face.

She was an only child and Menka was the center of her existence. When he struck her—the only time, my mother said, that he did so—he bent her spirit toward him for the rest of her life. She adored Menka as if he had been Brando himself, and she hated him with suppressed, embarrassed fury.

Even when she was in her late thirties, married with two children and living in a house in a New Jersey suburb, a withering look from Menka could turn her from a wife and mother into a little girl. She would freeze and start to stammer. By then my grandfather, about sixty-five, looked ten years older. A lifetime of heavy smoking had given him emphysema. He would start to cough, and cough and cough, then gag and choke, unable to breathe until, with a long, heavy, paper-crinkling sound, he heaved up liquid like a flame from deep inside his lungs. At moments like that, his eyes bulged almost out of his head. His dark-complexioned face turned a deep red. Tears—from his mortal cells, not from his emotions—ran down his face.

I did not understand how my mother could be afraid of such a weakened person. But Menka hadn't just struck her. As my mother told the story, he followed his blow with a short speech about all actresses being whores. He knew that for a certainty, he said, because he had encountered many actresses in the hotel. In that one instant, he thwarted my mother's ambition and tried to stifle the sexual yearning he felt inside it. In its place, he put a picture of his own sexuality in her head, stuck there, forever, with the adhesive of the slap.


Like the smell from a gas leak, money began to seep its way into every aspect of their relationship. If my mother wanted money to buy herself a new dress, Menka said no. If she wanted money to travel before settling down to marriage, he said no. When she met my father, an aspiring jazz pianist, Menka warned her against him because of his modest income.

With regard to my father, my grandmother drew a line. She insisted that my mother follow her own heart, and Menka relented. Rose seemed to spend most of her days in submissive silence, perfecting the art of the pot roast, but all the while she was discreetly consolidating her power over a husband who was outwardly aggressive yet inwardly meek.

A short, solidly built woman, Rose held her cigarette with an elegant delicacy that was like the tip of a submerged, different, commanding self. Simply holding her cigarette in such a way, she announced to the world that, despite appearances, she had ownership of Menka. Every once in a while, when she thought there was a battle worth fighting, she threatened to leave Menka if she didn't get her way. My grandfather always had weak lungs, suffering from asthma and bronchitis and then emphysema, yet he continued to smoke. The thought of having to fend for himself without Rose made Menka panic.

Roused to anger, she would insult Menka in Yiddish. The old words, bristling with consonants, left her mouth as though she were spitting out the broken bones of a small animal: *Vern zol fun dir a blintshik, un di kats zol dikh khapn*: "May you become a blintz and be taken by a cat." Cats made Menka struggle to breathe. He begged her to stay, often through tears, and gave her what she wanted.

I was an asthmatic child myself, prone to lung ailments throughout my life. I remember many times as a small boy awakening in the dead of night, whimpering and gasping for breath during an asthma attack. My father would rush into my bedroom in his underwear, sweep me up into his large arms, and hurry with me into the bathroom, where he ran the shower as hot as he could until the steam, and also my father's comforting presence, enabled me to breathe again. At the age of eleven, I caught pneumonia. My mother doted on me, and I grew accustomed to being cared for. Laid up in bed and swaddled in blankets for weeks, sometimes months at a time, I watched television and read the armloads of books that my mother brought me from the public library. Hemingway's *The Sun Also Rises*, which transformed a patch of sunlight on my bedroom wall into pitiless and romantic Spain; a compact volume titled *Understanding the Great Philosophers*, where I read about Spinoza, who supported his cosmic thoughts with a meager living as a lens grinder; an anthology of Greek tragedies told in the style of children's stories that held me rapt with figures who were unaware of how their conscious actions were weaving a countermotion to the fate they took for granted—these were some of my favorite books. I inhabited the real and made-up lives I encountered and pretended that on account of my heroic or poignant actions all the world revered or felt for me, and wished to care for me the way my mother did.

Once I was well, though, I felt vulnerable in a different way. I had to fend for myself without anyone to care for me. I craved the attention that I had received while sick.

Soon I found a way to reclaim the importance I had enjoyed. I discovered that I could make people laugh. Comedy conferred on me something like the power I experienced in my sickbed bouts of vicarious action. The sharper my distress, the more compulsive my routines.

One of my bits of business, which I developed around the age of fifteen, took up the centrality of tears in my family. It wasn't just Menka and I who melted. Tears were the family lingua franca.

All that family blubbering—a joke I concocted when still a boy: I was born with a silver violin in my mouth: yuk, yuk, yuk—rose up from dark places. It was blatantly manipulative, a tried-and-true gambit meant to induce guilt, but more elemental, suddenly crying was a way of coaxing someone into caring for you. During long bouts of illness, when I would read or watch television in marathon sessions, I sometimes sat rapt before the spectacle of Harpo Marx unmanning himself by putting his leg in someone's hand.

My routine, devised for my friends, went like this. I pretended to be one member of my family, and then another.

> The first member wrinkles his face and makes quiet
>      weeping sounds.
> The second member does the same.
> First member begins to sob.
> Second member sobs in response.
> First member weeps, and sobs and moans.
> Second member: ditto.
> Both family members weep, sob, and moan. Then they
>      nod their heads and embrace.

My routine incited the immoderate laughter of my friends: Paul Dolcetto, Alex Tarmanian, Teddy Di Buono, Terry Cushman, Peter Camino, Arthur Teitelbaum, Matthew Cassidy. They were all, like me, products of immigrant grandparents and white ethnic parents who had made their way out of New York City in the 1950s and 1960s. My friends had become my surrogate family, a home away from my increasingly turbulent real home.

It turned out that Menka's worries about my father were not unfounded. Unable to support his growing family on his pianist's slender income, but also eager to make a fortune in the booming real estate market that was rippling through postwar New Jersey, Monroe gave up his career as a jazz pianist and got a job as a realtor. About ten years later, the market collapsed, and after a couple of years of growing tension at his job, he was let go.

Unable to find another position in real estate, my father returned to music. The opportunities had narrowed for him there, too. Though in his prime he had played with the likes of Stan

Kenton and had never wanted for work at various nightclubs and swank private parties, he now settled for doing bar mitzvahs and weddings with his trio. He called himself Lee Sage when he was performing. To make ends meet, he gave piano lessons. It thrilled him to have a student who lived next door to Sam Sinatra, cousin of Frank.

One minute my father was composing songs that my mother had written the words for and sang while he accompanied her on the piano, the two of them recording their compositions in a studio at their own expense in hopes of hitting it big—the next minute my mother was at his throat, accusing him of negligence, incompetence, all sorts of weakness.

My father's own father, Leopold Siegel, died of a heart attack at the age of forty, when Monroe was thirteen. This left my father permanently heartbroken. He stuttered until he was in his twenties. Throughout his life, he became tongue-tied in moments of stress. He could not stand up to my mother.

Despite my father's crooked teeth, he was a tall, handsome, good-natured young man who seemed to regard the future with a confidence nourished by his creative gifts—besides being a pianist, he was a natural painter, self-taught, though he never thought of art as more than a hobby. My mother the aspiring actress would have fallen for his artistic side. And for the fact that my father utterly lacked Menka's malice.

But more than anything else, it was mutual vulnerability that drew my parents to each other. Sharing faltering parts of themselves that needed to be supported reassured each of them that the other was incapable of inflicting pain. It would not have occurred to them that, at the same time, a race had begun to see which one would become exhausted by the other's weaknesses first.

Here, as in just about everything else worldly and practical, my mother had the advantage over my father. They were both sentimental people, but my father was sentimental, period. My mother was too adept at manipulating her emotions to allow them to have the last word over her.

My father often talked about a traumatic event that occurred when he was a child. He grew up in a recently constructed white colonial in Mount Vernon, New York, a suburb just outside New York City. His family had a dog, a German shepherd named Rex, that they sometimes kept tied to a tree in the yard. My father loved him. One day someone cut the rope and made off with the dog. Whenever my father recalled what happened, his face took on a kind of stricken wonderment.

I never knew whether Rex was taken before or after the death of Monroe's father, but marveling over the mystery of the missing dog, again and again, was Monroe's way of grieving over his father while trying to suppress the memory of his father dying. My mother, on the other hand, was indifferent to animals. Perhaps it was because she could not perform for them.

In those moments when my mother berated him, my father would cry: *Hab rachmones!* which is Yiddish for "Have mercy!" My father knew about four words in Yiddish, and those were his two favorites.


My mother's increasing unhappiness with my father turned her into a different person. She screamed at me over my slightest infraction. Modest requests that I made, like being permitted to stay up a little later, or asking her to drive me to a friend's house, or even to allow me to have a friend over for a visit, she denied me with a gleam of malicious defiance in her eyes. Discontent with my father's slowly worsening situation at his job seemed to bring out the Menka in her. I fell into the category of disappointing child. It was around then that she began to get physical with me in her anger, something I had never experienced with her before. It made me wonder whether she was telling the truth when she said that Menka only hit her once.

She never hit me in the face. She hit me on my arms and legs, preferring to slap me on my bare legs whenever she burst into my bedroom and caught me partly dressed or naked, in which case I hurriedly threw my blanket over myself in mortified rage.

In these scenes with my mother, which started when I was about fourteen, I surrendered to hysteria, sobbing and struggling to breathe, the way I had learned to give myself up to fever when it arrived with all its accompanying luxuries of care, attention, and dispensations from my everyday obligations. My only defense against my mother was to implore her in this way to mother me again.

Instead she yelled and continued to slap me. Her eyes flashed with Menka's malice, and also with defiance of her own self-loathing. This made her hate herself even more, which fueled her defiance, and on and on, until she whirled away. She disappeared into her bedroom and slammed the door. I was left with red marks on my legs and arms.

During my mother's slapping fits, I would pretend to be standing outside of myself. I invented an inner voice that I called the Old Man. The Old Man would comment on the scene with detachment. "She is hitting you," the voice would say. "She is trying to scratch you. She is screaming at you. She is leaving the room." By transforming these scenes into a kind of living story, I felt that the world was witnessing what I was passing through. Imagining that I was commenting on my experience for other people, the way my cherished authors wrote for other people and for me, made me feel less miserably alone. The ability to lose myself in the parallel worlds I found in books, and especially the joy I felt in coming up with my own ideas about life, became my deepest consolations. From that time on, intellectual reverie established itself as my favorite mode of escape from painful events and thoughts.

•

My father bore the brunt of my mother's rage. She spit at him and tried to scratch his face. They became less like people and more like acting and reacting inanimate objects repeatedly colliding with each other in space. In my horrified eyes, material worry reduced them to scrimmaging chunks of matter themselves; to things. As if in an effort to recover his humanity, my father often fled from my mother's wrath to the den of our small split-level house. There he spent hours listening to his modest collection of recordings of jazz pianists: Art Tatum, Teddy Wilson, George Shearing, Oscar Peterson, Erroll Garner. Garner he prized above all the others.

What distinguished Garner was his percussive left hand. While other pianists used their left hand to seek out complicated chords that added depth and dimension to the melody, Garner's left hand supported his melodies with a constant rhythm. He caressed, stroked, or pounded the piano with it. There was a joy to the way the steady, percussive left hand made the melody buoyant, propelled it upward. It was a joy that seemed to rise from Garner's loins.

Garner began to play the piano at the age of three and never learned to read music. When he was eleven, he started playing on riverboats traveling the Allegheny River, and by fourteen, he was performing in nightclubs. For him, playing the piano was seamless with existence itself; his work was his life, and his life was his work. Somewhere my father shared Garner's joyous self-fulfillment. You could see it in his glowing face when he sat down at home to play the piano, an old stained and nicked dark brown spinet that we kept in the den, a narrow room just down a flight of stairs from the kitchen. Perhaps this simple fulfillment ex-plains why Monroe was so happy whenever he returned from a modest gig in a cavernous banquet hall somewhere. Even giving lessons seemed to cheer him. He didn't seem to register the fact that he was scarcely making enough money to support us. He was playing piano. This is partly what drove my mother into her violent frenzies.

A depressed person, my father was easily transported out of himself by strong appeals to his senses like Garner's music. His depression was rooted in the fact that pleasure filled his head with dreams of happiness and success. Once life imposed its demands, rigors, and restrictions, he retreated with sadness into himself. He needed the self-affirmation that pleasure briefly affords. Without that, life was just too hard for him, and he almost automatically resigned himself to setback and disappointment.

One of the ways I occupied myself, during long spells laid up in my sickbed, was to read book after book about the Holocaust. It became an involuntary passion; an escape from my sickness by immersing myself in an unfathomable disease of human nature. A passage in one of the books buried itself in my imagination. An SS officer distractedly mutters to a Jew he finds annoying, Why don't you just kill yourself? The inmate shrugs his shoulders, finds a corner somewhere, away from the SS man who is no longer even aware of his existence, and hangs himself. My father, broken by his own father's death, seemed not just to shrug but to nod in satisfaction when he lost his job, and when he began to lose my mother. It was as if he had always expected those things to happen.

My father and I watched Laurel and Hardy movies on TV together on rainy Saturday afternoons, my head resting on his stomach. Knowing how much I liked to hear the ticking of his watch, inherited from Leopold, he placed his hand over the side of my face so that I could hear the inner motions of the watch. While I listened, he gently stroked my face. Laurel and Hardy made my father laugh so hard that my head heaved up and down on his stomach as he roared. He adored slapstick. The spectacle of physical calamity that had no ill or fatal effects delighted him. We bought a slot car together and raced it at a place in a neighboring town once or twice a month. I was surprised to see how skillfully my father managed the turns at high speeds. Pitching for my Little League baseball team, I could hear him cheering me on, despite the fact that he knew nothing about baseball or about any sport. He was intimidated by athletic contests that fostered hard certainties about who should win and who should lose. Still, I could hear him yelling as I hurled the ball: Go, Lee-boy! Strike 'em out! You can do it, Lee-boy!

Gradually, though, he slipped from my grasp. His weakness, the way he fled from my mother, the fact that he could not fend for himself out in the world—all of that embarrassed me. Embarrassment, no matter how much I tried to suppress it, led to pity, and pity, no matter how hard I fought against it, incited my contempt.

I was fourteen when one afternoon on my way home from school I was confronted by two bullies. I was riding my bicycle near our house on an overpass that spanned Route 17. Our house was situated right off Route 17, which ran north into New York state and south toward New York City. I often walked to the overpass at night and lingered there. When it was clear, you could see the Empire State Building. The soaring obelisk's spire was illuminated at night. During the day, it trembled in a blue haze.

That afternoon one of the bullies planted himself in front of me. We were all in the same junior high. I used to see them around, always together, always apart from everyone else. They wore denim jackets over white T-shirts: at the time, the outsider's equivalent of a prep-school blazer.

One was blond, the other had dark hair. They would have

been handsome, but nature had betrayed them. The first had dark red splotches on his cheeks, beneath high cheekbones. A giant brown pimple had grown on the fine, aquiline nose of the other.

I could have ridden straight into the boy who stood in front of me, but I might have knocked him into the road and the oncoming traffic. So I braked and stopped. The other boy came up close to me and butted me with his chest. The boy in front of me grabbed the handlebars of my bike and began to push and pull the bike. You're a stupid faggot, said the one who was next to me. Each of them grabbed one of my arms. At that moment, Monroe drove by in his Buick Electra. All I had to do was wave and cry "Dad!" and they would have given me one final push and slouched off. But the possibility that my father might stop the car, walk over, and try to help me filled me with terror. I had an image of the two boys beating him. So I smiled and waved.

My father, I confessed to them after he had safely passed. The two bullies looked at me in surprise. Faggot, said one. Wuss, said the other. They pushed me a few more times and left. When I got home, my father grinned and patted my shoulder with affection. Your friends look like nice boys, he said. I'm glad you were having fun.

Around this time, my father, a big man, with thinning brown hair, crooked teeth, and bespectacled light blue eyes, was starting to flounder. His large frame began to sag with despair. The experience of my large father suddenly becoming vulnerable haunted me. Yet he proceeded as if his material circumstances hadn't changed. He had some sharply tailored suits left over from his days in real estate that he liked to wear. He continued to indulge a weakness for expensive shoes, of which he had several pairs. Every year, as he had when he still worked as a realtor, he leased a gleaming new Buick Electra. The car was one step down from the Cadillac he dreamed of but never had the money for.

He barely had the money for the Electra, either, but that didn't stop him.

All these small boosts to his self-esteem belonged to the happy, oblivious piano-playing Monroe. The real Monroe could no longer afford them. One night my mother went into his closet, pulled out several pairs of his shoes, and confronted him. She threw them at his face, one after the other. He stood before her, transfixed by her rage. I hated her for humiliating him, and I hated him for allowing himself to be humiliated.

Burdened by stress, some people garden or take up photography. My mother went berserk. In these crazy bouts, there was not an impulse that she did not act on. There was not a sentiment that sprang into her mind that she did not express. *Ya zig moi, vrog moi*, the razor-tongued Menka liked to say in Russian. "My tongue is my enemy." By means of hysteria, my mother turned herself into a riveting presence. Her hysteria was a plea for help, but it was also how she controlled her environment. Flying apart was how she kept herself together.

At the age of twelve, I broke my leg skiing at night with my junior high school ski club, at a place called Sterling Forest, just over the border in New York state. The binding didn't release when I fell. My leg broke in two places; a spiral fracture wound its way up half of it. The ski patrol arrived in a cloud of flying snow. They bound me to a sled and raced with me down the mountain to an ambulance. By the time I got to the hospital the middle of my leg below the knee had swollen to the dimensions of a grapefruit. Numbness was giving way to pain. Orderlies rushed me on a gurney to a table in the emergency room, where a nurse began to cut away the leg of my pants.

Enter Lola. The conscientious, if unwitting, ski-club chaperones had called her to report my accident. I watched her with dread as she stood, timidly at first, in the doorway. Slowly her attention revolved from me to the emergency room's bright lights and small audience of doctors and nurses. I began to moan to myself. I knew what was going on inside her head.

Paramount Pictures Presents
*A Mother's Ordeal*
Starring
Lola Siegel
Introducing
Lee Siegel as "The Son"
With
A crowd of handsome young doctors, any one of whom could play the leading man in Lola's next feature film,
*Say You're Sorry!*

*Lola enters the hospital emergency room. Her striking brown eyes flash as she looks around for her son. There he is, lying on a table, wearing the same torn and filthy sweater he has been wearing for two weeks. People say Lola looks like Mary Tyler Moore. They are wrong. She is a dead ringer for Jennifer Jones. Maybe Loretta Young. But not Mary Tyler Moore.*

LOLA
(*touching her stunning coal-black hair as she flies past an admiring young physician*)
My son, my son! What have they done to you? What have these vicious ski-club people done to you?

LEE
(*clearly confused by his pain*)
Mom, please.

LOLA
Oh, my son, my only son!

LEE
(*confused and disoriented*)
What about Nathan, Mom? My brother?

LOLA
Try not to talk, my darling. (*Suddenly she becomes alarmed.
Turning to the nurse, she exclaims:*) Do you have to cut his
pants? They are the only pair he has that are clean and
without holes!

LEE
(*transformed by his selfish adventure into a thankless child*)
Mom, please leave!

(*Lola's heart begins to break. She turns to the doctors and nurses.
She bursts into tears.*)

LEE
(*to the nurse*)
Could you get her out of here? Please?

LOLA
What drugs have you given him? This is not my child!

(*Lee turns away and moans softly.*)

LOLA
(*clutching her heart*)
My son is in pain. I can't breathe. Let me sit. Will he be
able to walk again? Will he be able to make a living?
Oh, I feel dizzy.

THE NURSE
(*a vicious, envious little bitch*)

You'd better wait outside, Mrs. Siegel.

*(Sobbing quietly, Lola begins to exit the room. She stops.)*

LOLA
*(addressing herself to the evil nurse)*
I will be in the waiting room all night, if you need a
transfusion. *(She pauses. Then she faces the doctors and
nurses.)* Or a transplant!

*Lola returns to the waiting room and lowers herself into a
chair. Soon she is brought a glass of water by a young doctor
who looks like Keir Dullea in* Madame X, *the finest movie
about a woman ever made, after* Joan of Arc. *She tells the
young doctor, who has exceptionally straight teeth, the story of
her life. He is moved beyond belief.*

Original behavior, like my mother's, is hard to resist. If you are
dependent on it, as I was on my mother, you experience it as a
type of power. And power awes. Whoever is being subjected to
power makes no distinctions between the different forms of
it. Power that has its origin in strength is indistinguishable
from power that has its origin in weakness. I shrank into myself
before my mother's helpless jet streams of emotion. Still, they
imprinted themselves on my reflexes.

For all her embarrassing or painful conduct, my mother
embodied an attractive alternative to my father. In contrast to
his weakness, she displayed strength. As my father's inability
to earn a living diminished his power, my mother's emotional
flights dominated our household. My weak, histrionic mother
was power incarnate.

My father came home from the office one day with terror on
his face. I heard him tell my mother that some of the men he
worked with had been taken out in handcuffs. This was nothing

new in the Walpurgisnacht of New Jersey real estate. People were getting arrested all the time. As I learned later in my life, the real estate industry in Jersey was rife with the fraudulent sale of trust deeds, forged escrow instructions and forged grant deeds, and the use of nonexistent buyers to purchase properties.

But my father was an innocent. He had strayed from the realm of making music, where he had given and received pleasure. That was the only world that he felt comfortable in. You walk into a room and sit down at the piano. Two other people enter and take up their positions behind a string bass and a set of drums. You play apart while at the same time playing together. No one expresses himself at the expense of someone else. No one can express himself without the collaboration of someone else. Even if you have a dead father dragging on you like cement shoes, you have the safety net of intertwined melodies below you.

Suddenly Monroe found himself in a world of calculating hardness. He found himself in business. Instead of collaboration he encountered collusion.

My socially uncertain parents rarely entertained, but they once had a small dinner party for a man who I assume was either my father's boss or someone he worked with whom he had to impress. The honored guest was dark-suited, all starched white cuffs and collar. His watch and cuff links flashed under our tarnished brass chandelier. Under the light, his short, wavy black hair, controlled with gel, gave the top of his head a shiny, corrugated look. His face was genial, fleshy, and tan.

My younger brother was sequestered in his room as usual, obsessed with his coin collection. I wanted to come down, I guess I was about ten, to say good night to my parents.

We lived in a modest split-level, at the top of a dead-end street that ran up a hill. A split-level is just that; not two floors, but one floor split into two. Neither is an actual floor since they are separated by a staircase consisting of a mere three steps. A split-level is really two halves of two different houses.

I had picked up the names for different types of houses by hearing my father talk about them. My father loved the terminology of real estate. Leopold's death had forced Ann, Monroe's mother, to sell their white Mount Vernon colonial, and selling real estate for a living later offered my father the illusion of controlling parcels of the precarious physical world. The fact that he was a mostly ineffectual realtor made no difference. Music came too easy to him. A little boy who allowed his dog to be taken from him, who permitted his father to leave him forever, didn't deserve an easy time of it. Sweating, laboring, forcing himself against his nature to sell real estate was the way my father punished the little boy that he had been. Leopold, in fact, had been a realtor.

You enter a split-level house through a brief foyer that runs into the kitchen, which overlooks the backyard. To the right of the foyer is the living room. Situated perpendicularly to the living room, and connected to it, is the dining room. The bedrooms are off a short hallway to the left of the foyer that begins at the top of three steps. My brother's bedroom was first, on the left, across from the pink bathroom he and I shared. My parents' bedroom, with their own bathroom, was farther down, on the right side, at the end of the hall. My bedroom was at the very end.

I went downstairs and my parents introduced me to their guest and to his attractive blond wife. I have forgotten their names. They were warm and pleasant to me. I must have been wearing my favorite pajamas. Red with black piping, they consisted of a button-down shirt and loose pants. The picture of a panda bear with its mouth open, probably meant to indicate a yawn, appeared on the shirt pocket. I never changed them. The pajamas must have smelled of sweat, sleep, and dried urine. He's adorable! the special guest's wife exclaimed. My mother fluttered over me and my father smiled. I made my way back upstairs to my room.

Once there, I turned off the light and jumped loudly into bed. My brother banged on the wall in protest. He seldom spoke because he had inherited my father's stutter. In his mysterious nighttime chamber, he worked out the first stages of his destiny in coins, then drums, then weights and martial arts.

I lay still in my bed. After a few minutes I quietly opened the door. I made my way past the pink bathroom on one side, and my brother's den on the other. Carefully I perched at the top of the stairs. That was the place from where I would customarily eavesdrop on my parents.

I recall hearing my mother talk and laugh, and the guest and his wife talk and laugh. My father, who never drank, was mostly silent. Alcohol probably would have pushed his emotions out of him like rain melting snow off a roof in heavy chunks. A drink or two and all his pain would have tumbled down. But one sip of wine made my mother giddy.

Finally the evening took the turn for which I had been waiting. The two couples moved into the living room for "cake and coffee." The plastic had come off the green silk sofa that my mother had saved for years to buy. Two armchairs, newly re-upholstered with gold-embroidered, dark blue velour, stood on either side of the sofa. When I heard my parents and their guests rise from their chairs, I withdrew to a spot in front of a closet that was at a ninety-degree angle to the pink bathroom. I could sit there, hidden from view, and now and then snatch a glimpse into the living room.

I could barely make out what they were saying, or make sense of what I heard, but I saw them clearly enough. My father and the special guest's wife faced each other from across the room in the rehabilitated chairs. The special guest and my mother sat at either end of the green silk sofa. At one point, the guest bent his glossy head toward my mother as if he couldn't hear her. She emitted a laugh that had been loosened by the wine and laughed again. With a playful smile, he bent his head once more. My mother rose and sat down beside him.

Sitting with their knees touching, my mother and the special guest talked in hushed whispers, broken by regular intervals of shared laughter. My father and the special guest's wife sat in their armchairs, on either side of the sofa. After a while, my father fell silent, his eyes cast toward the floor. As an adult he often grew silent when in younger years he would have stuttered. I wondered why he wouldn't look at my mother or try to join their conversation. He sat there awkwardly fingering his glass of what I assumed was ginger ale.

By contrast, the special guest's wife sipped her drink in comfort. She gazed around with an air of superior detachment at my parents' tentative approximation of middle-class culture: a copy of Renoir's *Woman at the Piano* that hung on the wall across from the large picture window; two oil paintings that my father's mother had given to my parents and that had been placed over the sofa: both, from different perspectives, of a narrow street winding through an old city until it disappeared into the shadows. The twin pictures depressed and frightened me when I was a boy.

The broad, soft chest that I laid my head on, Leopold's gold-plated watch, twice beloved, by Monroe and by me, the long, beautiful, fragile-strong fingers on the hands that applauded me with happy ignorance of the sport I was playing—my father's bulk rested inert on one of the embroidered armchairs while my mother bent her head toward the special guest, crossing and recrossing her legs until her skirt slid up the middle of her black-stockinged thigh.

My father took these social gatherings at face value. He enjoyed my mother's exertions in the kitchen and the meals she cooked. He was grateful for her outgoing manner. It distracted people from his timidity. Her extravagance even endowed his diffidence with a flattering possibility—if Monroe's wife is so intense, Monroe must satisfy her nature somehow.

My father thought these evenings could win him friends. Perhaps that misperception was why he didn't have any. No, Dad! Protect yourself! Harden yourself! Gird up thy loins! Your special guest is a coldhearted son of a bitch who wants to rip you to pieces. He wants to eat you. He wants to devour you and then slip his hand, with its diamond ring and gold watch, between Lola's legs. And all the while his wife, perfectly composed, even cheerful, will be pretending, with that freshly acquired air of cultural superiority, to be interested in the name of your upholsterer.


Growing up without money, my mother entered Hunter College, part of the city university system, determined to become a teacher. She needed a way to make a living. But like many people drawn from a young age to a vocation that is never realized, she kept the possibility of being an actress alive even as it was becoming more remote. The waiting itself became a comforting habit.

Our happiest times as a family were those occasions when we assembled a little band, with my father on piano, my brother on drums, me playing the electric bass guitar, and my mother singing. My mother closed her eyes and belted out the songs with a gutsy, Shirley Bassey voice that bounced back and forth between the narrow den's thin walls: "What Kind of Fool Am I" and "More" were favorites, along with some ballads that she and my father had written together.

Slowly, gradually, she reduced her theatrical aspirations to make them fit into the life she was living. I never saw her teach, but from time to time, other kids who had been in one of her classes told me how much they had enjoyed her, though whenever anyone began to talk about her as a teacher, I wanted to run away rather than risk a glimpse of my mother through someone else's eyes that might have made me cringe.

My mother was part of a wave of first-generation American women, the daughters of mostly European immigrants, who found work in public education after the war. They had to support themselves while they looked for husbands or helped their parents out. In rare situations, a steady income was necessary for those women who had chosen an independent life.

In my mother's case, she lived at home with Menka and Rose, contributing to the household expenses. She met my father on a blind date. She waited for him while he went off to the Korean War, where he served in the artillery. Upon his return, they got married. A few years later, they moved first to a garden apartment in Bergenfield, New Jersey, a working-class suburb, where I arrived, and then to the split-level house in Paramus, a mostly lower-middle-class borough with some pockets of modest affluence, about twenty-five miles northwest of Manhattan.

My father never graduated from college. For years I believed him when he said that he had gotten his bachelor's degree from the City College of New York. After he lost his job, my mother told me that he had been lying. When I confronted him with what she had said, he turned away. I didn't pursue it. He looked too wounded by the exposure of his lie. I could not bear his wounded look.

Money was a good part of the reason that my father gave up music for real estate. On the most basic level, he could not make enough money with his music to support a family. But there were emotional forces driving him, too. Though not Hollywood-obsessed like my mother, who sat sobbing through the Academy Awards every year, my father had his own movie playing in his head. Leopold had had some success as a realtor before he died. If my father felt that he deserved to fail as punishment for his father's death, he was also driven to follow in Leopold's professional footsteps as yet another sacrifice to his father's memory.

My father worked at Albatross Realty. After a few years, fortune smiled on him, and they elevated my father to vice president. For the first time, my parents were flying high. We undertook a series of, for my parents, extravagant vacations, each one more exotic than the last: Philadelphia; Washington, D.C.; Fort Lauderdale, Florida; and, the ultimate destination, the Virgin Islands.

My brother cured his stutter on that last trip. Slipping out of the hotel room he and I were sharing, which was adjacent to my parents' room, he walked out onto the terrace joining the two. He returned with what would become a permanent grin. He had seen my parents having sex, and in some sort of reverse trauma he never stuttered again. He simply stopped talking altogether, except for talking when he had to, and making snide remarks, through that strange rictus of a grin.

My father, in the manner of a man of leisure, took up a hobby: photography. Suddenly he went from being someone worked on by the world to someone recording the world. His creative gifts had given him, beneath the insecure withdrawal, a touch of aristocratic confidence. There was the way he handled those sharp turns at high speeds with such aplomb when racing slot cars, for example. In that glorious season of his life, his innate gifts, which had been buried under all his flaws and misfortunes, bloomed.

Our house itself took on, in my eyes, magical dimensions. Not long before, I had seen Laurence Olivier's *Hamlet* on public television, and though I had trouble understanding the play, I had absorbed the movie's enchanted chiaroscuro through my pores. Now the new atmosphere of happiness and fulfillment transformed the split-level into a castle, with long corridors, stone walls, battlements, and a keep, out of which came, late at night, my parents' laughter.

Meanwhile, my father's newfound contentment was imposing a tariff on his fate. In hindsight I can see the catastrophe coming.

Nature had given my father beautiful hands. The sight of them enriched your impression of him. They were the hands of a born pianist—he had perfect pitch—and playing piano was where he found all the pleasure in his life.

One Saturday afternoon when I was about twelve, sitting in the kitchen having lunch, I heard my father scream. It was an anguished, horrified, animal shriek. Trying to put up a shelf in the garage, my father had hit his thumb with the hammer. The nail was shattered and his thumb swelled to the size of a pinecone. I heard the scream, and I saw him run up the stairs to my mother in the living room with a look of astonished helplessness on his face.

The second portent occurred a few summers later. I wasn't home at the time. My father was mowing the lawn. At one point, he noticed that the lawn mower was no longer cutting the grass evenly. Tilting it over, he saw that a wad of leaves had gotten caught in the blades and he decided to remove it. Incredibly, he did not turn the lawn mower off first. He thought that if he was careful, he could catch hold of the edge of the clump of leaves that was sticking out of the blades and tug on that to get the whole thing out. The lawn mower lopped off the tip of one of his fingers.

When I got home, he was sitting in the living room, in one of the gold-embroidered, blue velour armchairs, his hand bound with surgical tape. The mound of bandages wrapped around his finger made it look like an animal's paw. It was weeks before he was able to play piano again.


"Money," wrote the Dutch philosopher Spinoza in the seventeenth century, "has presented us with an abstract of everything." Money embodies the power to purchase and to own. It is the consummate medium for the human desire to possess: territory, objects, even other human beings. Money puts everything within reach. The problem then becomes how to acquire money.

Since the essence of being human is to desire, and money is the universal medium of desire, then every exertion, or enervation, of intellect, will, and emotion eventually becomes an economic event. That is why the back of the dollar bill has a picture of an all-seeing eye suspended over a pyramid. All creation submits to the dynamic of money.

Freud famously believed that the way you have sex is a revelation of your personality. I would amend that. Your relationship to money is also a revelation of your personality. The way you handle money and the way you have sex are mutually illuminating.

Yet I have often wondered if money is a natural feature of human existence. Would there be the equivalent of money in any world, in any universe, the way there must be the equivalent of oxygen anywhere there is human life? Or is money as the abstract of everything an artificial abomination that human beings must contend with, weary generation after weary, beleaguered, exasperated, fed-up, infuriated generation?

Albatross had my father on what is known as a draw. I don't know anything more about the arrangement than that. I don't know if all the brokers were on a draw, or if my father had any choice in the matter of how he was paid. All I know is that the company paid my father a certain amount of money every week against his future commissions. The idea was that he would pay back the money that had been advanced to him out of the commissions he received from the deals he closed.

This worked for a while. Like the Platonic form of Beauty, from which is derived our instances of mundane, earthly beauty—a painting, a full moon, a face—my father's and therefore my parents' happiness derived from the Draw. The Draw recalled a novel I read as a boy about a magical "wild-ass's skin," which allows its owner to fulfill his wildest dreams but shrinks after each dream is fulfilled. In my father's case, the more he depended on the Draw to live, the more it shrank his life.

I once felt the power of the Draw the way Moses felt God's power in the heat of the Burning Bush. In the mid-1960s, when I was about seven or eight, I emerged from my bedroom in the middle of the night, intending to make my way to the pink bathroom to relieve myself of excess water.

The castle was still. Not a sound was there in the long, stony corridor. I heard nothing except, now and then, the sound of clinking coins emanating from the bedrooom of my brother, the younger prince. He liked to remove his ducats from the slots in their folders at night to count them. Outside, the courtyards, the stables, and the woods beyond were silent. The servants were abed.

My bedroom, that of the eldest prince and heir to the throne, lay at the end of the corridor. The stronghold where my king and queen slumbered was situated next to mine. I slipped out of my chamber. As I was turning around after gently closing the door, I nearly bumped into the king as he was exiting the royal boudoir.

His face was red and sweaty. His features were slightly distended. Stretched across his face was a smile that I had never seen on him before. It was a frank and uncomplicated expression of pleasure, rooted so deeply and confidently inside him that when he saw me, he didn't flinch or draw back in surprise.

He was so absorbed in the cause of his smile that he encompassed me in its warmth. He glanced at me while still smiling, but smiled right past me, as if our near collision was part of the flow of his current happiness.

I looked down and saw that the boxer shorts he always wore

to bed had something like an outstretched hand beneath their front. He turned away, still smiling to himself, and proceeded to the pink bathroom. My mother must have been using the one in their bedroom. I returned to my room tense and bewildered.

The Draw brought out my father's and mother's natural endowments. Our little band convened and played more often. Monroe and Lola composed more and more songs. The Draw hovered over Monroe and Lola while they made love.

The Draw resembled the force of love itself: binding, expanding, rooting. It projected the illusion of permanence onto a crumbling, uncertain world. It was like Athena casting an aura over her favorite warriors on the Trojan plain.

The Draw was exactly that: a drawing-out. It extracted the excellent and rare qualities of my parents that circumstance and serendipity had all but obliterated. Of course their own human weaknesses contributed to the obstruction of their gifts. Yet I have always wondered if my father's infirm will and lack of confidence would have had a different outcome if money had not been the means by which they produced their effect. My father's guilt and self-doubt would have obstructed him in any universe. But whatever forces of character and circumstance determined my father's relationship to money, money was the decisive factor in everything that came to pass. In a universe—or a society—where money was not so gravely consequential, would his personality have destroyed his life?

Perhaps Monroe could not be blamed for taking, and taking, and taking the Draw, even as his commissions dried up. To finally be what he wanted to be was the most normal circumstance in the world. If the Draw was what made it possible for him to be happy and to support his family, then, in his eyes, the Draw was a natural condition. Lola, who for the first time began to accept the place where she found herself in life, even if it was composing songs and performing them at home, embraced her husband's faith in the future.


Kindness, theoretically speaking, begets kindness. The next time you are standing behind your overloaded cart on line at the supermarket, invite the quiet, thoughtful young man waiting behind you with a bottle of Coke and a Snickers bar in his hands to go ahead of you. When he bursts into the movie theater where you are sitting with your wife and children, shooting people in their seats with a semiautomatic rifle and seven handguns, he might recognize you and allow you and your family to live. People often remember the nice things that you do.

Alas, cruelty responding to cruelty is more of a certainty than the reciprocity of kindness. The push on the playground or in the bar provokes a counterpush. Onerous terms of surrender at the conclusion of a war guarantee a second war. A slight, once embedded in someone's mind, metastasizes into rage. The pendulum of getting what you give has a bright side, too. Daring all might lay, after an excruciating period of suspense, the world at your doorstep.

Energy spent is always energy exchanged. The action in the Garden of Eden, even if it was lying around all day looking at the sky, had to have a reaction. God would have eventually cursed Adam and Eve and their descendants with the punishment of laboring in the sweat of their brow even if Eve had not disobeyed Him. You have to pay up sooner or later.

As it turned out, waiting for Adam or Eve to defy Him and display their autonomy as persons was a stroke of genius. God was saying: for this good thing, autonomy, you have to trade another good thing, autonomy in a different degree. Thus was born the eternal law of something given, something taken; something taken, something given.

My father proceeded as if that law did not exist. In this, he was one of two things. Either he was a child, a blind, clueless, Eden-person, unaware that, as a poet once wrote, "in dreams begin responsibility"; obligations accrue; debts must be paid. Or he was—absurd as it sounds given his mildness, defenselessness, and incompetence in practical matters—a descendant of Lucifer, the angel who rebelled against any trade-off or exchange that would diminish what a person truly was.

In the 1970s, the interest rate for borrowing money reached the highest levels in American history. With no money available to people who needed to take out loans to buy a house, the real estate market collapsed.

Of course the wealthy could still purchase a house without a mortgage loan. Through the blessing of inherited wealth, for example, something similar to the Draw continued its elevating influence, though the exchange of energy in the case of inherited wealth—something given, something taken; something taken, something given—is obscure.

But for everyone else, the great uplifting that had powered America after the Second World War, thanks in part to the GI Bill, which had enabled my parents to buy their house in the New Jersey suburbs, came to a halt.

Interest rates went up. Male erections came down. Women who depended on men for pleasure and procreation went unfulfilled. The fate of tens of millions of men and women hung in the balance as President Nixon tried to persuade his chairman of the Fed to substantially lower interest rates.

The president's efforts were unsuccessful. By the mid-1970s, the birth rate in America was the lowest it had been in modern times. The tools Nixon put in the hands of his Watergate "plumbers" were like the president's own desperate attempt to keep himself at full mast. When I see footage of the American flag being taken down over the American embassy in Saigon in 1975, I think of Nixon, Watergate, birth rates, and my father.

The commissions stopped coming, yet my father took, and took, and took the Draw. Either he felt life owed it to him, or he felt that he owed it to himself and to his family, obligations and/or consequences be damned. One way or another, he had unconsciously devised a catastrophic revenge on the little boy who lost so much without lifting a finger to stop it. Within a few years, Monroe accumulated fifty thousand dollars in debt, which is equivalent to about three hundred thousand dollars now. When he couldn't pay it back, and after a couple of years of lowering, raising, and then again lowering the amount of the Draw, Albatross fired him.

Monroe returned from work on the day he was fired from Albatross and sat down to dinner at our kitchen table as usual. I was about sixteen. Because my mother was quiet, we all ate in silence. My father must have given her the news earlier in the day, or in private, upon arriving home. Nathan, who rarely spoke by that point, usually sat in such a slouching way, darting his eyes around, that you felt he was communicating something, if not actually taking part in the conversation. But that night his posture and expressions were neutral.

We finished dinner, still without speaking. My father was eating the grapefruit my mother had wordlessly served him for dessert when, all of a sudden, he began to weep.

I had seen him cry before, every year in fact, on the Jewish High Holy Days, as he stood in the synagogue to say Kaddish, the prayer for the dead, for Leopold. Throughout the ten-day span of that holiday, he wept intermittently. He would run downstairs every couple of hours, even in the middle of the night, to check on the flickering Yahrzeit candle he had set up on the kitchen counter in memory of Leopold, to see if the flame had been extinguished. It was like making sure his beloved Rex was still tied to the tree. His annual spells of weeping made me shrink even more from him. But I associated his displays of emotion with the pathos of the holiday, so I was not overpowered by them.

That night, however, I sat aghast as I watched the tears roll down his cheeks. Grapefruit was my father's favorite dessert. He relished eating it. Now his face was wet from the grapefruit's juices and from his tears.

My mother went to him and put her hands on his shoulders. Monny, she said, using his nickname, everything will be all right. Then, as if feeling that she had fulfilled her function or satisfied an obligation, or perhaps experiencing the same startlement and revulsion that were sweeping over me and my brother, she stormed upstairs in a hint of the histrionics that she would fall victim to, and indulge in, for the next few weeks.

Most real estate companies that have their employees on a draw rather than a salary are prepared to eat their losses. For whatever reason, Albatross came after my father for the money.

Maybe it was too large a sum for them to simply write off. Maybe my father had overstepped a boundary and they were getting even. Maybe he had crossed someone there. (The seductive man with the corrugated hair!) It could have been that Albatross itself was endangered and they were attempting every recourse they could to stay afloat. But for whatever reason, Albatross pursued my father with implacable force. Unable themselves to collect the money my father owed, or to get it through the efforts of a court officer once they had obtained judgment against him, they passed the debt onto the sheriff's office in Bergen County, New Jersey.

The doorbell rang one afternoon a few months after my father's breakdown at the dinner table. A stranger was standing there when I opened it.

Now it was not Bill the Mechanic, with his rheumy green eyes, who smelled pleasantly of grease and motor oil, and who flirted with my mother in a high, squeaky voice. It was not Larry the Butcher, who also smelled of his work, of the fresh meat he delivered in crisp brown paper, and who was too shy to flirt with my flirtatious mother. Instead he spoke to her with a knowing, leering smile that was the way he concealed his shyness when dealing with female customers.

Nor was it my favorite presence at the door, Dr. Etra, who came to the house whenever I had one of my annual attacks of flu or bronchitis. His iodine smell meant that effective protection had arrived. Dr. Etra was short and rotund with a beefy face. He looked like Fiorello La Guardia in the pictures I had seen of him. When pneumonia raised my temperature to just over 105 degrees, and I felt that I was hovering outside my body, and that my skin had the sensitivity of an open wound, he stood a few feet from my bed, speaking in low tones to my distraught mother and father. Passing in and out of consciousness, I clung to the sight of his solid stockiness, his baggy black pants flooding his oversize black shoes. The heat had made my mind grow hands, beautiful hands with strong fingers, and with the new prehensile warmth growing out of my throbbing brain, I hung on to Dr. Etra's bulk and pulled myself away from the oblivion that was enticing me toward it.

These figures were reliable people in our suburban life. They were creations of economic relationships that grew into half-business, half-personal relationships. They were both the guardians and the fruit of our stability. The stranger standing before me that sunny spring afternoon in a long white raincoat was an abrupt break with everyday reality. He was the product of a broken economic relationship with the world.

He slowly took his hand out of the pocket of his raincoat
and showed me his badge, which identified him as a Bergen
County sheriff.

Like many American boys, especially at that time, I had absorbed
into my conception of myself the idea that, on some level, I was
a law-enforcement officer. Deep down, I felt that I was the typ-
ical cop or detective of American popular culture. At war with
his superiors, he had to break the departmental rules in order
to enforce the law.

The cops of movies and TV, and also the sheriffs of West-
erns, were really ingenious versions of American adolescents who,
in their minds, were at war with their mothers and fathers
and had to break the family rules in order to enforce the laws of
romance, gratification, adventure, Musketeerian solidarity, and
so forth. At the age of sixteen, I wanted to belong to society;
I wanted to belong to everything, everywhere; I just wanted to
belong in my own intractable way—all the more intractable for
my discomfort about being, deep down, open to everything and
everyone. On the small or big screen, the appearance of a badge
signified to me that the person brandishing it had, so to speak,
invented his own conformity. The real badge being flashed at
the top of our front steps had the opposite effect on me. It was
a denial of my actual life.

The sheriff processed me with hard, hooded eyes. With a
smirk, he brushed past me into the castle without telling me
why he was there or waiting for me to invite him in.

I started to tremble. An encounter with power has an effect
similar to a car accident. All at once, it wakes you up from the
daily slumber of familiarity and routine, and it causes you to
feel that you are inhabiting a dream.

To change the terms of your existence: that is real power.
What the sheriff's badge and his twinkling, apathetic eyes meant

was that everything that mattered to me was of no importance out in the world.

He went past me along our short foyer into the kitchen. He walked with a slow gait, taking his time, glancing into the living room to his right and then up the three steps down the hall toward the bedrooms on his left.

These places had grown to giant dimensions for me. His scrutiny made them look puny. The castle, with its turrets, and long hallways, and winding staircases, and mysterious bedchambers, dissolved into a white split-level house on a dead-end street that was separated from a car dealership and hissing Route 17 by a decaying gray stockade fence.

As for the sheriff, well, he was no Wyatt Earp or Matt Dillon—they were real lawmen. This man had a drinker's veined, bulbous nose and pink splotches on his pasty white skin. Not to mention that smirk. Real sheriffs, that is to say, Hollywood sheriffs, never smirk.

The stranger walked right past me. He moved along the foyer with a brutish intimacy. Years later I hated it whenever a cop who had pulled me over for a traffic infraction adopted a sudden intimacy with me and called me by my first name. School-yard bullies use your first name to mock you. The sudden intimacy of the police aims to obliterate the familiar emotions that you depend on to structure your life. It is a threatening intimacy meant to demolish the sympathetic bond on which genuine intimacy is based. "Tell me, Lee, why were you going eighty miles an hour in a forty-miles-an-hour zone?"

I followed the sheriff as if he was the new master of the house. In fact, new terms of ownership were what his deliberately unhurried gait implied. Our home was his if that was the course the law decided to take. It was obvious that my father did not have the money to repay Albatross. So the firm demanded his assets. These, aside from his shoes and clothes, consisted of the split-level house that my parents had bought in the first flush of parenthood and economic success, as they moved out of their rented apartment in Bergenfield. The court had sent the sheriff to serve my father notice that it had a legal right to seize the house on behalf of Albatross.

The sheriff entered the kitchen and continued to look around. He took in all our major appliances. This included our refrigerator, onto which my mother, a walking compendium of treacly sentiment, had stuck one of her favorite inspirational tidbits: "I once had no food to eat / Then I met a man who had no teeth / I once had no shoes to wear / Then I met a man who had no feet."

The cop had preserved his smirk, in much the same way that Nathan had preserved his grin. Seeing him turn his smirking face toward the poem whose vulgar sentiment made me wilt whenever I saw it was too much for me. I could not endure the shame I felt.

I decided to attack him and, if necessary, to kill him.

Everything happened in a blur. He turned toward me and began to speak. A crow made its raucous sound somewhere. Out of the kitchen window I could see a dog bounding in freedom across the backyard, his leash flying behind him. I grabbed the sheriff by the lapels of his raincoat. He punched me in the face. I pushed him into the refrigerator and gripped his neck with my hands. Wrapping my fingers around his neck, I began to press on his throat. "Say you're sorry, you little prick," I said. He tried to knee me in the groin, but I placed my leg alongside him and flipped him over it. He hit the ground with a thud. "That poem has a lot to teach us about life," he said, as he struggled to raise himself off the floor. I thought for a minute. I replied, "The creation of art has nothing to do with the inability of the artist to fulfill an obligation unworthy of his exceptional gift." I then drove this important point home by walking behind him and kicking him in his balls just as he was getting on all fours to lift himself off the ground. He shot forward, his head slamming into our aging dishwasher. His lifeless body slumped to the floor. Now I had to figure out how to dispose of the corpse. I knew Nathan needed money to buy some more rare coins. If I gave him twenty dollars, he would probably help, though I wasn't sure. You could never tell what mood Nathan was in.

As all this action was unfolding deep inside my head, the sheriff asked me where my father was. I was still trembling. I don't know, I said.

Where is your mother, he said softly.

Out, I said. Food shopping.

He regarded me with his hard, hooded eyes.

Where is your father, he said.

He's out, I said.

Where, he said. He didn't ask questions. He made statements that demanded answers. But he did it in a soft voice.

He's out working, I said. He teaches. He teaches piano. He's out giving a piano lesson.

The sheriff took a white envelope out of his raincoat pocket. He now spoke in such a low tone that I thought I heard kindness in his voice. I began to imagine that another form of protection had arrived, that he was there to help us keep our collapsing household from falling completely apart. All that TV and movie watching had instilled in me a demented romanticism. His low and gentle tone meant only that he had attained the apex of his power in his little visit to our home. He did not have to go to any effort to destroy us.

What's your name, he said. His smirk had given way to a travesty of a smile.

Lee, I said.

I'd like you to do me a small favor, Lee. I have to hand this envelope to your father myself. That's the law. He gave a faint shrug, as if to say, "The law is as much a pain in the ass for me as it is for you." Then he continued to smile into my eyes, as if to say, "I bet you wish that was true."

But, he said, if he's not here, I can't give it to him, Lee. Do you understand that.

Yes, I said. I do.

Good boy, he said. You just tell your father that I was here, okay.

I nodded. Okay, I said.

He smiled one last time, walked back down the foyer without waiting for me to lead him out, and left the house.

My mother came home carrying bags of groceries. I helped her put them away. After that I told her about the sheriff. She gave me a pained look, to show me how much my father was making her suffer. Then she rubbed her hand up and down my upper arm. Don't worry, she said. Everything is going to be all right. Yeah, yeah, she sighed to herself so that I would hear her. Her eyes began to moisten.

These days she wanted only to win me to her side, partly to hurt my father, and partly because, even in her wildest furies, she still felt a sentimental attachment to me.


That autumn, a few months after the sheriff's visit, I was playing basketball in our driveway. My friends and I had put up a backboard and hoop. Though I could not dribble the ball to save my life, I was a fair shot. I spent hours shooting hoops well into the night, when I turned on the naked bulb that years before someone, I had no idea who, had wired to the front of the garage.

I had just come back from school. My mother wasn't home. Because my father's income from his piano lessons and the few performing gigs he and his trio were able to get was not enough to support us, she had returned to the elementary schools as a substitute teacher.

She usually had three- or four-day stints at a time. The Paramus Board of Education would call her early in the morning to tell her that she was needed and to ask if she was available. She always was, unless she was sick as a dog, which was not an infrequent occurrence for either of my parents. They were both chronically depressed and often down with a cold or the flu. On the mornings when my mother got the call informing her that there was an opening, she roused herself from the heavy, underwater slumber of those depressed people who sleep too much rather than too little, shuffled downstairs, and, gradually, after one cup of coffee that was mostly milk, and a bowl of cereal, went off to work.

I returned from school and had my customary snack of cherry pie that my mother had picked up for me at the supermarket, and a glass of Coke. Then I retrieved the basketball from the garage. I started to throw the ball toward the net. Imagining that I was playing with friends, I shouted out their names as I pretended that I was passing them the ball and they were passing it back to me.

I was especially attached to Paul Dolcetto. Paul lived with his mother, stepsister, and stepfather in a bigger and newer split-level house on the other side of town. His mother had divorced his father, a sanitation worker, when Paul was a child. She remarried a gum-chewing captain in the Tenafly police department named Danny Clementino, who disciplined Paul with a blackjack.

Paul played his electric bass guitar with the concentration of a chess grandmaster. He suffered from constant nosebleeds. He laughed until his nose bled, moaning, No, no! Stop! Enough! I can't breathe! He responded to the beatings from his stepfather, he told me, by charging him, kicking and throwing punches.

With his steep forehead, receding hairline even as a boy, and long, prominent nose cursed with its mysterious wound, he looked in profile like the image on an ancient Roman coin. The broad, steep forehead he got from his mother. The striking

nose and the defiant spirit he must have inherited from his real
father, whom I never met, the garbageman who, I imagined,
threw bags of trash into the garbage truck with a noble, blood-
racing fury that he suppressed with an effort of concentration.

My other friends had made it clear to me in various ways,
and not without awkward affection, that they did not have the
emotional intensity I wished to share with them. I depended
more and more on Paul. We shared a love for the bass guitar,
for one thing. The bass stays hidden in the background but
supplies an indispensable rhythm. On some level, that is how
we thought of ourselves. Invisible yet indispensable.

After school I would ride my bike over to Paul's house
with some of my father's Erroll Garner records. I placed them
in a carefully folded shopping bag that I put in the basket that
hung from the handlebars. My father never knew I was borrowing them. Paul would listen with me to Garner playing "I'll
Remember April," "The Shadow of Your Smile," "How High the
Moon." As Garner swung and bounced and grunted his way
through those songs—grunting as he played was his trademark—
Paul listened intently, his head down, that grandmaster's absorp-
tion in his light gray eyes. He understood Garner. That meant
that he understood my father, which meant that he grasped the
bond between my father and me.

I loved him for that. I opened up to him about the disorder
at home, divulging every detail. He listened sympathetically. He
put his hand on my shoulder to reassure me. My mother screams
and slaps me the same way yours does, he told me. They're crazy.
Crazy and unhappy.

Together we plotted to take revenge on the county sheriff if
we ever saw him. After a while, his mother would walk to the
door of the basement, where we held our meetings, and scream
down to us to come upstairs for milk and cannoli.

In return for Paul's sympathy, I entertained him by mocking
the police captain. I imitated his small-time swagger and the cop

stare that he would train on Paul beneath heavy-lidded eyes. Drop the cannoli and take the gum! I would cry, playing around with the famous line from *The Godfather*. The romantic gangster epic had opened that year and its spectacle of outsiders under siege established it at the center of our imaginative lives. I had quickly assimilated Brando's performance, trying to summon up his menacing cool during those times when my mother went on one of her slapping rampages against me.

Thinking of home, enraged at my mother, I did Danny as the ridiculous villain of a goombah police captain. Paul laughed until the blood flowed. Extracting a tissue from the reserve he kept crumpled up in his pants pocket, he held it under his nose as he leaned his head back over his chair. The white tissue slowly became soaked with blood. He might have been a dandy sniffing a rose in a Victorian photograph. It pleased me to see him vulnerable in this way. I felt that it guaranteed his friendship.

But a few days after one of these Danny-bashing sessions, Paul would boast about Danny's associations with gangsters. He spoke, with excited admiration, of Danny's violent exploits in enforcing the law. Danny himself, on more than one occasion, went looking for the older boys who had been pushing Paul around after school. Drawing up next to them in his patrol car, he introduced himself, which always solved that particular problem. Paul hated his stepfather, yet he worshipped him, too.

Since it was important for me to have solidarity with someone all the way through, this disconcerted me. It cast a haze between us. In response to Paul's ambiguous status, and to my other friends' inability to be available to me whenever I needed them, I found myself wanting to spend more and more time alone. Frequent illness had made me comfortable with solitude, even reliant on it as a way to allow my mind to wander in safety through fantasies of fulfillment.

•

That autumn afternoon I lost myself in shooting hoops in our driveway as the leaves drifted to the ground around me and the light began to weaken. My father pulled up in the brown Buick Electra, parking it on the street in order to allow me to continue playing ball. He waved to me as he walked down the driveway. I waved back. My father stood off to the side of the driveway, watching me. The sharp, aching light was vanishing quickly, as if its brightness had been an illusion.

Too awkward and unsure of himself to make friends, alienated from his younger brother, who regarded Monroe with derision, estranged from his brittle mother, who had never recovered from her husband's early death, driven away by my mother—hammered and banged up, he stood at the edge of the driveway, regarding me with longing.

I saw him standing at the edge of the driveway in one of the expensive suits he used to wear when he was a realtor. The pathos of him going to one of his lessons dressed in that extravagant suit stung me. He must have seen the discomfort in my face, but not the pity. Pity was what he was in need of. He walked over to me.

How are you, Lee-boy, he said.

I'm fine, Dad.

You look great. A strapping boy.

Thanks.

My strong, strapping boy. Do you have a minute?

Yeah.

You're quite a ballplayer.

I just like to shoot.

You make every shot.

No I don't. I miss a lot.

Well, you make almost every shot.

I miss a lot, Dad. Anyway, the net is like only nine feet high. Remember? We messed up when we put it up. It's tilted now, too.

Ah, that doesn't matter. You're having fun. Do you want me to help you straighten it out?

No, it's okay.

Come over here. Let me help you.

No, it's okay.

Come over here. Help me push it straight.

No, Dad. Come on. You're wearing your nice clothes.

Heh, your old man isn't so bad, is he? He's not so terrible to look at.

Yeah.

What do you think? Do you think the girls would give a second look at your old man?

The post is okay the way it is, Dad. It's always been like that. It doesn't make a difference.

Do you have a girlfriend? You must be fighting them off.

I know a few girls.

I bet you do. They must be following you around school.

Not really.

What?

Not exactly.

There must be someone special. Is there someone special?

No. Not really.

Well, that's fine. The important thing is to have fun. To meet people. Then you find the right girl. You have plenty of time.

Yeah.

All the time in the world.

Yeah. Yeah.

You should go out for the basketball team. You're a natural.

I can't even dribble.

But you can shoot.

Lots of guys can shoot.

Just keep practicing. You'll make the team.

I'm not interested, Dad. I just like to shoot.

I think the ball needs air.

It's okay.

It's not bouncing right.

It always does that in the cold.

Are you cold? Do you want to go inside?

No, I'm fine.

It's going to snow soon. We're going to have a bad winter this year.

I'm not cold.

Did your mother take the car?

She hasn't come home yet.

Did she go to the store?

I don't know.

Is she still at school?

I'm not sure.

Sometimes she likes to stay late at school. She grades papers, talks to people. She loves to talk. To meet people. She works hard, your mother.

I guess.

No, be nice. Your mother works hard.

I am being nice.

We might fight, but she still loves you. You know that.

Yeah.

She just gets frustrated, but she loves you. You and your brother are her whole world.

Yeah. I know.

She'll be home soon.

Yeah.

Can I talk to you?

Well, yeah.

I want to talk to you about what's going on between me and your mother.

Okay.

We've been fighting a lot lately.

Yeah. It gets pretty bad.

I know it does.

She's, like, screaming at you every night.

Your mother screams when she's upset.

But it's, like, every night.

We're going through a bad time now.

It's pretty bad.

We're going through a bad time. But everything is going to be all right. Your mother. Me. The house. Everything. It's all going to work out.

She screams at me and hits me for no reason. Why does she do that?

I have to tell you something, Lee-boy.

Yeah. Okay.

Can we talk for a minute?

Yeah, Dad.

I'm going to start sleeping downstairs in the den for a little while. Just for a little while. To help make the peace with your mother.

Wow. Where? On the couch?

It will just be for a little while.

Wow. What does Mom say about that. Dad? What does Mom say? Dad, don't cry. Dad, please don't cry here. We're outside. Please don't cry.

Your mother is in a lot of pain.

Well, then maybe you should stay in your bedroom with her.

No, this is what we're going to do now. I have to make the peace. She's in so much pain.

Don't cry, Dad. Jesus Christ! For Christ's sake!

I can't have sex with your mother anymore. I'm not able to have sex with her.

What?

I can't have an erection. I haven't had an erection for about a year.

What? I don't understand. What are you saying?

That's why I'm going to sleep downstairs, Lee-boy. It's easier for your mother. It's easier for both of us.


People had called Leopold Lee. For that reason, my father had a hard time just calling me by my first name, so he often played with it. Lee-boy was his favorite pet name for me. But appealing to me was a way to recapture the old—so old in my father's memory as to be mythological—"Lee." That night he poured his heart out to his father's ghost in the form of his living son.

His confession was the final assault on my fragile sense of self. It must have been in that moment that I began to develop my habit of defining myself in opposition to other people. I feared that if I surrendered to this weak, childlike man I would disintegrate. I envied Paul Dolcetto his blackjack-wielding stepfather. That was a person Paul could fight. It is much harder to defend yourself against a destructive weakness that is pleading to be saved and understood.

Opposing my father, angering him, whipping him up against me made him, at least, strong in my eyes. The following summer, on a weekend down the New Jersey shore, as I passed by him while he was standing on the fourth-floor terrace of our motel, leaning his elbows on the railing, I grabbed his shoulders, gave him a push, and then pulled him back again. His angry face, when he turned around, gratified me.


By the time Menka embraced me under the bright coin of a moon that late August night before I went away to college, mournfully asking what "she" was doing to us, my father's crisis with Albatross and the sheriff's visit to the house had made my mother resolve to leave my father.

Meeting another man had been the catalyst behind her

decision. He happened to be the principal of one of the elementary schools where she was teaching. He had a sonorous Sicilian American name: Angelo Bonanno. The only real problem, beyond the painful but unavoidable logistical hurdles on the path to divorce, was Menka.

Menka had a practical attitude toward marriage that made him disapprove of divorce as the practical response to a failed marriage. He considered marriage to have little to do with happiness. Marriage provided the axis from which happiness could be pursued. Once married, you had a companion whose material and biological interests were aligned with yours. This meant that you had the blessing of someone you could trust in matters of life and death.

Through the years the two of you established a common heritage, by means of which your identity maintained itself. Creating a countermotion to life's erosions and disruptions in this way, you could continue to push back against the iron boundaries of existence by extending your vitality through children.

There was no such animal as romantic love, any more than actually flying with your lover to the moon, if that were possible, would be anything less than a big physical and emotional letdown. What people called romantic love was perseverance with another person in the face of rising and falling disappointment, for the sake of safety, relative power, stability, effective functioning, and sporadic pleasure.

Marriage was the only form this haven could take. Marriage was the way you carved out of the alien world a familiar world, something you recognized when you opened your eyes in the morning, the way you wake up and see the same sky, clouds, and sun every day.

For Menka, an existence without marriage would have been a world where the paper-thin membrane of sky, clouds, and sun did not exist, a world where you spent your days running through the darkness, away from alien rocks hurtling toward you out of icy, indifferent outer space.

But no one can stay rational about love and all the arrangements that have been constructed in its name. Rose stood in the way of Menka's liaisons with prostitutes and struggling actresses at the hotel. Yet without Rose, he was lost. So Menka turned to money.

He lavished presents on Rose. Half his income went to the prostitutes and the actresses, and the other half went to his wife. He showered Rose with trinkets, some of them valuable, left behind in the hotel that he passed off as gifts that he had bought.

Rose was under no illusions about where Menka's bounty came from. But it didn't matter. Menka's thoughtfulness, even if it was the product of guile, put her at the center of his life. The fact that his gifts were really appeasements, and that these were transparent, and that he knew she knew about them even as she pretended that she didn't, gave her an extra power over him. The marriage continued not because Menka wanted it to, but because she allowed it to. He was the one making all the exertions, not her. On his part, Menka made a great display of his exertions, taking pride in what he believed was their effectiveness.

In this way, each one thought he or she had the power over the other. But it was Rose who could instill terror in Menka simply by leveling at him a proprietary gaze while elegantly stubbing her cigarette out in an ashtray.

So when my mother told her parents that she was divorcing my father, Rose said nothing to oppose it, while Menka considered it a disastrous step to take.

For one thing, women didn't upset the apple cart like that. The vicious world outside of marriage was hard enough for men to deal with alone. My mother would find herself in the position of the indigent actresses he had known at the hotel, not just the young women struggling to succeed, but the older ones, washed up and washed out, alcoholic and alone. That fate was what he had tried to save my mother from when she was a girl.

True, he had opposed the marriage to Monroe, a point that I heard my mother remind her father of over the phone when Menka was obviously lashing out at her over her decision to leave my father. On the phone, or fighting with her father on his visits to our home or on ours to his, whispering with her mother in another room so loudly that my brother and I could hear every word, Lola handled her pain the only way she knew how, by performing it so that everyone, friend or foe, became part of her crisis.

Still, Menka reminded her, Monroe had come through in the end. They had a nice house in the suburbs, far from the crime-ridden city. They had two nice children, though the oldest child locked himself in his room playing loud music and stayed out late drinking with his friends. But that, Menka admonished my mother, was her fault, for letting the marriage get so out of hand that she had no time left over for her sons.

If Monroe had stumbled—as Menka once predicted he would—at least he had learned his lesson. Already he was begging her not to leave him, vowing that he would return them to the solid financial footing they had once enjoyed.

My mother's retort to her father was simple and based on the following facts:

After the sheriff's visit to our house, my father announced to my mother his plans to use some legal maneuver that he might well have imagined to take out a second mortgage on the house. This way, he explained, he could fulfill his obligation to Albatross and get out from underneath the debt that was crippling them. They might, he added, even have some money left over to take a vacation, or buy a new car for my mother.

This was too much for my mother to tolerate. Thanks to my

father's run of good luck when the real estate market was booming, they were only a few years away from paying off their original mortgage. Taking out a second mortgage would rob them of equity that would be available to them in their retirement. It would endanger them for a second time, placing a sword over their heads much like the Draw.

But my father was insistent, exuberantly making his case. He was itching for a second chance. It was several years since he had replaced the Electra with a new model. The sleeves on his suits were beginning to shine with wear. His shoes were buckling in at the toe.

It wasn't just the pressures of his past and an escapist imagination that were driving him toward yet another disastrous decision. The artist in him, the pianist and the uncompleted painter, needed freedom from restraint. His human wealth required just enough money to remove the encumbrances on his spirit. Out of the welter of self-destructive impulses came these healthy promptings that he could not have been aware of or able to put into words, but that were as much a part of him as his guilt and self-doubt.

He possessed another superlative quality, too. He was kind. Other men, the men he had worked with in real estate, got rewarded for their coldheartedness, and often for their dishonesty, while he, Monroe Siegel, who had never hurt and would never hurt anyone, had to groan and stumble through life simply because he could not operate at a similar distance from his feelings. Did not kindness deserve an income?

After several months of tense calm, during which my father continued to sleep in the den, his new plans pushed their marriage into its terminal phase. This time there was no hushed whispering in what was now my mother's bedroom, followed by her screams and my father's retreat. The fighting occurred all over the house, at all times of night and day.

The last thing my father wanted to happen was my mother

leaving him. For all his excitement about his idea, a few days, or even a few hours of objection from my mother would have convinced him to back down. Amid my mother's yelling, my brother and I could hear him saying, Maybe you're right, and, We could wait a while if you want. He was clearly about to reverse himself. But whenever he seemed to yield, my mother escalated her attacks on him.

She was not going to let the opportunity pass. The very fact of him wanting to take out a second mortgage was the proof of my father's detachment from reality that she needed in order to finally say goodbye to him. Her nerves had rejected him a long time ago, then her flesh. But her conscience needed something more solid.

She instinctively knew that she required an error of judgment so plainly rooted in my father's character that she could console herself with it in times of regret, or on those occasions when someone lifted a reproachful eyebrow as if to say, "You reap what you sow." Most of all, she had to have irrefutable proof of my father's lack of responsibility to his family so that she could present it to Menka, whose opposition to her divorce from my father must have reminded her of his opposition to her desire to become an actress.

For those reasons, my father's openness to her objections incited her to greater fury. She was not going to permit him to escape back into the marriage by complying with what she wanted. What she wanted was no longer anything that he could give her.

In my mother's eyes, the qualities that he thought warranted a dispensation from the world's hard consequences—the qualities that once assured her they would have a future together—were the gates of hell. Behind my father's kindness, she saw denial, weakness, selfishness, and vanity. His plea for her to have *rachmones* she regarded as a challenge to her existence, a death threat.

Once he left their bed, everything was over. His sojourn in the den was her Purgatory.

Or so I imagine.

Within months of my father proposing a second mortgage, my mother asked one of her cousins, the husband of one of Menka's nieces, a high-flying divorce lawyer in Manhattan, to file for divorce and get my father's name off the deed to the house. It was a tricky process, but he was a skillful lawyer. Not long after that, my father was out of the house and my mother and Angelo were openly involved, though Angelo did not move in for a couple of years, until his and my mother's divorces were finalized.

Did my father know about Angelo and, if he did, was that the true motive behind him wanting to take out a second mortgage? Would the new burden of debt, in both his and my mother's names, have proved her commitment to the marriage if she had agreed to it? The material constraints it would have imposed might have guaranteed her fidelity, or at least her caution.

The son of Sicilian immigrants, Angelo had grown up in a strict Catholic household in industrial Paterson, New Jersey, about twenty minutes away from Paramus. Defying his family's working-class suspicion of intellectual pursuits, he resolved to become an educator. Not just a teacher, but an educator. He was the first person in his family to graduate from college. He was also one of the few Italian Americans of his generation to earn a Ph.D., which he received in the field of education.

As soon as I learned from my mother that Angelo was going to supplant my father, I plotted with Paul Dolcetto, who claimed to know about these things, to kidnap Angelo from his elementary-school parking lot and break his legs with my Louisville Slugger—Go, Lee-boy! You can do it, Lee-boy!—thus persuading him to reconsider what he was doing to the castle and the royal family. But I came to my senses.

My mother told me that she liked Angelo because he took everything in stride. With his steady, observant eyes, he did create a calming effect. He had a naturally broad chest but delicate features: arched cheekbones and thin, flared nostrils. A chain smoker, he suffered from a persistent cough. The delicate facial features atop his broad chest seemed precarious when he coughed, like a pyramid of crystal champagne glasses balanced on a wobbly metal table.

The truth was that he was holding it all in. Ten years after taking up with my mother, he was dead of a heart attack. Angelo's Irish-Catholic wife had lost her mind, in a tempest so destructive that a New Jersey judge took the unusual step of giving Angelo full custody of their three children. He had whisked them away, without a second's hesitation or doubt, to the alien sanctuary of my mother's split-level house. Angelo handled stress with a Sicilian sense of fatality.

So while he busied himself in the kitchen, cooking delicious southern Italian dishes like braciole, my mother applied herself to his children in her characteristic way. Regarding them as obstacles to Angelo's loyalty, she demonized them by pretending that they were pawns of their mother.

Trying to preserve himself for his children, Angelo maintained his outward serenity in order to spare himself and turned a blind eye to my mother's cruelty toward them. When my mother caused the children to cry by feigning disgust with something one of them said, or by disparaging his two daughters' appearance, Angelo would put his long arms around Lola and the wounded child, say, There, there now, and try to calm everyone down. This made his children hopeless. On their daily visits to our house, they moved around like wraiths, which left Lola with a satisfied gleam in her eye. Angelo, a gifted cook, returned to the kitchen shaking his head yet smiling to himself as he worked.

With me, Angelo practiced the same careful self-preservation. After my initial belligerence toward him, I weakened, as I always did before men who seemed to possess a strength that my father lacked.

He was not like my father, who was good at bursts of enthusiasm with me—cheering me on, racing slot cars, watching movies—but bad at the long haul of talking with me and trying to figure out who I was. My whole immersion in the world of high culture, of books and classical music, had gone almost unnoticed by my father. Monroe was too beset by professional and personal difficulties to be able to focus on the specifics of my life. He tried to make up for that with shows of affection. Hugging me and kissing me, he would tell me how smart I was, how funny, how cut out I was for great things in the world. Then he would withdraw wearily into himself and disappear in plain view.

Angelo, eager to establish harmony in the house, detected my hunger for someone to share my passion. One of his first gestures was to buy me *The Norton Anthology of Modern Poetry*— the first edition, now out of print and a collector's volume. I was over the moon. His communion with me touched me deeply. That book and I became inseparable. Its gossamer-thin pages, crowded with words that could not be reduced to words, dense with intuited meanings that conferred a special distinction on the person who apprehended them, lifted me above all the desperate whispering, shouting, and conferring around me.

Occasionally I would read a poem to Angelo. He would listen intently, wait until he caught my eye, and merrily raise his eyebrows to display a bond with me. I don't think he ever connected with the poetry because it would have required him to abandon his cheerful detachment. But he enjoyed watching me grow closer to him.

I loved reading him one particular poem, written on the occasion of a young boy's birthday. He listened to the last stanza with an affable smile:

Happy Birthday, Johnny,
live beyond your income,
travel for enjoyment,
follow your own nose.

However, my mother soon grew threatened by my attachment to Angelo. She began to reel him into her conflicts with me. Whenever this happened, he darkened and pulled back from me, as if something familiar deep inside him was striding forward to crush the life out of his heart.

As the place where blood and oxygen meet and are exchanged—the inside achieving equilibrium with the outside—the heart makes for a good Armageddon. I had no awareness of Angelo's fears, of course. As he maneuvered to preserve himself for his children, I shrugged him off and began to move away from him, as I had with my father.

Living with just my brother and me, my mother was free at last. But she was not happy. She had only one close friend, who, busy with her own family, could not ease my mother's loneliness and despair. She belonged to no clubs or groups. She had no money. She could not turn to either of her parents for support. Menka was of course out of the question, and Rose's support consisted mostly of not offering any resistance.

My mother was ill-equipped to become the person she wanted to be. In the same way, there are people with no aptitude for math or science who dream of becoming doctors.

The distance between what my mother wanted and what she had the capacity to get for herself made her decision to leave my father all the more brave in her own eyes. It certainly didn't lack for courage, or prudence. Whether my father would have been able to get a second mortgage or not, the state of mind that made him resolve to do so would have jeopardized all of our futures. He had already demonstrated how irrational desperation was making him by using the money I had received for my bar mitzvah, including savings bonds meant to pay for my college education, to try to appease Albatross in his negotiations with them.

My mother felt she had no choice but to push my father out of the house. Yet she had not fully reckoned with the consequences. It had not occurred to her to weigh the difference between unhappiness within a marriage and unhappiness outside it. This is not to say that I think she should have stayed with my father. It is merely that there is only so much people can do to be happy, no matter what they think they should do.

Shortly after my father left the house my mother had a nervous breakdown. She raged and wept. The bedroom became her home within our home. It was convalescent room, crisis center, and bunker all in one. Reaching her breaking point in the course of the day or night, she would run into the bedroom and slam the door. Then she would lock it. She would stay in there, probably lying in bed, sobbing and wailing, sometimes for hours at a time.

I was sixteen when her implosions began, not old enough to drive, though old enough to flee the house toward the sanctuary of my friends. But so long as she was in crisis, I couldn't leave her. I withdrew to my room, where I maintained a vigil beside the anguish pouring out of the room next to mine.

Nathan had long ago made a separate life for himself in his own bedroom. We were not able to console each other. My mother was responsible for this impasse. An only child, she was threatened by the possibility of an alliance between siblings. She could not conceive of sharing our love. We had to exist as two distinct streams of loyalty.

But competition between Nathan and me was the minimum of what my mother was trying to stir up between us. She sought our complete estrangement from each other. You are my favorite, she would whisper to me, sometimes within earshot of my brother. I love you the most, you know that, she would say, with that gleam of sardonic defiance in her eye.

She might well have repeated the same sentiments to my brother, though from the way he regarded me with hatred and alarm, I doubt it. To make the wedge between us permanent, she would tell me, this time in his presence and without the pretense of hiding it from him, that I was smarter, better looking, and more popular than he.

This was as absurd as it was cruel. I was mostly doing poorly in school, while he was not, and though we both required braces, my teeth, unlike his, looked like wartime rubble. I also had a stubborn cowlick that you could have hung me from.

If I was more popular, he had a sense of self-possession that I mostly lacked. What little self-possession I had I hungrily extracted from books and movies. There in my imaginary world, I invented a way to survive and constructed an ideal alternative self. I possessed two selves: a self-hating one that had no rational basis for loathing himself, and this invention of a grandiose one whose exalted stature was imaginary.

Nathan and I both had to contend with our mother's tumultuous sorrow each in his own way. He grew closer to her but at the same time managed to keep his distance. I moved in the opposite direction. For all my resentment of her, I could not bear to hear my mother suffer. From time to time I'd leave my room, go to her door, jiggle the doorknob, and knock gently, asking her if she was okay. Go away, she would say, let me alone. Yet she would say it in such a way, with such a desperate, pathetic whimper, that my inability to escape was guaranteed.

•

With my brother occupying his own forbidding space, the hay-
wire sexual energy of both my parents gravitated toward me.
In her early forties, my mother had coal-black hair, dark brown
eyes, and a youthful figure. She really did look a lot like Loretta
Young. As she began to lose control of herself, and at the same
time to feel penned in by her new life in the old house, she turned
to me.

I would be eating a snack in the kitchen after coming home
from school. Suddenly she would appear in the kitchen doorway, wearing a new pair of tight jeans that she had squeezed
herself into. Sometimes she would be wearing a yellow baseball
cap that she had just bought. How do I look? she would ask me,
leaning provocatively against the wall.

Something in the metamorphosis that she had been counting on had misfired. All of her changed, not just the part of
her that she wanted to change. The old tendency to pity herself
for the way life had limited her became a new tendency to pity
herself for the way life starved her desires now that they had become unbound. No longer did she behold my sicknesses and
injuries and cry, Why is this happening to me? Now she saw
my youth and my gratifications and she cried, What are you
doing to me?

Whatever there might have been in her that was reenacting Menka's seductiveness with her, or taking revenge on my
father, or simply losing her grasp on reality as she related to me
the way she wanted to relate to other men, she had become, in
some strange permutation of her personality, a jealous rival
for the life that she wanted to live and that I seemed to be
living.

My adolescent brain was having a difficult time absorbing
my new, seductive mother. When I closed my eyes to try to sleep
at night, images of girls and of sex mixed with the sight of her

in those tight jeans, wearing her sexy little cap, leaning against the wall.


Fortunately I had begun dating. This had the effect of stabilizing me, to some extent. Tina Durrell was the name of the girl I was seeing. She was not my first crush, but she was my first girlfriend.

The more I looked to Tina for the emotional stability I was deprived of at home, the more I thought I loved her. Meanwhile, Tina mistook my reliance on her for a type of gallantry. This was because I expressed my dependence in the form of wanting to please her, by making her laugh, by encouraging her in her passions—she was a champion swimmer—and by consoling her in her endless conflict with her mother, who was given to manic flights and was raising Tina by herself after being left by her husband.

Ministering to other people's needs like this was a capacity I developed: the ability to soothe, reassure, and uplift people the way I wanted to be soothed, reassured, and uplifted. The difficulty came when I expected them to return my ministrations. I had fallen so completely for Tina because she did return my solicitousness toward her.

The upset at home had inflamed my skin, causing psoriasis to break out all over my body. I was ashamed of the gross unsightliness that started out as an itch that I scratched and scratched, until it became a red patch, then a red bump, then a small red dot. As I worked at it with my nails, the red dot began to bleed, finally cooling off and drying into little circles of pink and white scabs. On broiling summer days I would wear long pants and long-sleeved shirts to hide my wounds.

The first time I took off my clothes with Tina, my desire for her conquering the shame I felt over my body, she ran her fingers over the scabs. I love your pink dots, she said. She made me feel good about myself. I trusted her.

I lost my virginity with her one afternoon in my mother's king-size bed when my mother was out substitute teaching. I told her that I loved her while we were having sex, and I kept telling her, and I kept asking her to tell me that she loved me. She obliged in a low voice, dramatically, and with great delight, as if she was responding to my deepest emotional need, and not having sex with me at all.

One evening my mother stopped me as I passed her on the short steps between the upstairs and the downstairs hallways. She had been sitting on one of the steps. It was jarring to see her sitting there like that, in such a girlish position: knees up, arms folded across her knees, her chin resting on her arms. It was one of many jarring impromptu, young or girlish things she did at the time.

How is Tina? she asked. Proud to have a girlfriend, to be in an actual relationship with a girl, I had told her a lot about Tina. But I could see from that old malicious gleam in her eye that she wasn't interested in my new girlfriend.

She's fine, I said as I continued past her to the top of the three steps.

Are you seeing her tonight? she asked.

Maybe, I said. Maybe I will. Yeah, I guess so.

I bet the two of you have a lot of fun together, she said.

Tina is great, I said. I began to wonder fearfully if she had smelled the sex Tina and I had had in her bed a few days before. I wonder now if I had made love with Tina in her bed because I wanted her to smell it. I turned around and headed to my room at the end of the hallway.

I bet, my mother said as I walked away, that you are the biggest screw in town.

That night her physical closeness to me on the stairs and her words mingled with all the other bewilderments in my heated twilight thoughts. Though she never touched me, I started to lock my bedroom door at night.

At home, my mother, Nathan, and I were eating TV dinners in place of the elaborate meals my mother once made, even during the week. I didn't know whether this was because my mother lacked the money to buy food or because she was too depressed to shop and to cook. I did know that even with my father, by now living on his own, contributing to the household expenses, things were tight. Occasionally I would hear my mother on the phone with her one close friend, Judy Baum, say, amid fragments of hushed conversation, the words "food stamps." But I never knew whether she ever applied for them.

I had been working part-time since I was fifteen. Now my mother began asking me for, as she put it, "rent." Work was easy to find. The fact that New Jersey had no sales tax, along with Paramus's location at the intersection of two major highways— Route 17 and Route 4, which ran west and east and thus also into New York—had made the town a major commercial hub. In 1957, the year I was born, two of the largest shopping malls in the country opened up in Paramus: the Garden State Plaza and the Bergen Mall.

Even before she needed me to contribute to the household budget, my mother had believed that working while going to school would strengthen my character. Develop marketable skills, she told me, so that you will have something to support yourself with. My going off to work as a stock boy in a department store seemed to give her more pleasure than my modest accomplishments at school, where despite my lackluster academic performance I was winning praise from my English teachers for my "reading comprehension" levels.

Partly my mother was repeating Menka's mantra of having something to fall back on. As Menka's emphysema had worsened, his effect on her had weakened, despite his opposition to her desire to divorce my father. As he had become a more enfeebled figure, my mother seemed to take pleasure in defying her earlier fear of him by boldly adopting his worldview. *You have to make a life for yourself,* she also told me, parroting another of his favorite directives. But she was not just repeating Menka's sentiments. She was also stifling my ambitions as Menka had once stifled hers.

Yet the most disturbing element of her new relationship with me was the way I seemed to threaten her. One day, after we had a bitter fight and I told her that I was feeling dizzy, she snapped back at me, You'll end up outliving us all.

That night I called my friends to a summit meeting. Packed into Alex Tarmanian's tiny green Toyota Corolla, the marijuana smoke seeping out of the windows, all seven of us agreed that it was unusual for a mother to reproach her son for the natural fact that he would most likely outlive her, though as Alex intelligently observed a few nights later, after briefly speeding up a highway exit ramp in the mistaken belief that it was the entrance ramp, no one's longevity was guaranteed.

Maybe because my mother had the temperament of an actress, she assimilated the dynamic between her and Menka, her first and most commanding director, more seamlessly than most other children absorb their parents' influence. This was reflected in her seductiveness toward me, which would reach its peak of intensity a short time later, when I brought home my college girlfriend during my first summer back from college.

At the height of one of our pitched battles, when we had screamed ourselves out over some small thing—me glancing at a book at the dinner table, me wanting to go camping overnight with my friends—and we were standing there, red-faced, trembling, our voices hoarse with rage and emotion, my mother would pretend that she was having a heart attack. She would fall to the ground. There she lay, inert. This happened either late at night when Nathan had long been asleep or during the day when, for whatever reason, he was not at home.

The first few times my mother clutched her chest and dropped to the floor, of course I panicked. I shook her and shook her, but she would not respond.

Still naive about the most basic things, I had no idea where to locate her pulse. I could not bring myself to put my hand on her breast to try to find her heartbeat, so I placed my hand on her stomach until I could feel her breathe. Once I determined that she was still alive, though, I was at a loss. I thought of slapping her gently in the face as I had seen people do in the movies, but I could not get myself to do that, either.

I just sat by her motionless body, saying "Mom" over and over. I was no longer the boyfriend of Tina Durrell, or the budding intellectual who had won the praise of his English teacher, or the testosterone-driven teenager drinking and roaming the town with his friends, looking for girls. I was a virile young man suddenly robbed of his virility.

My mother repeated this scene three or four times until I caught on to the theatricality of it and pretended to call 911, which immediately resuscitated her before I could give the imaginary dispatcher our address. She seemed addicted to her simulations of dying. She would lie on the floor, often in her nightgown, with her legs spread out and her underwear showing. After a time, she would open her eyes and moan. Gradually sitting up, she would pretend to slowly return to consciousness. Where am I? she would ask, blinking, asking me to help her stand. Grasping her hand, I would support her as she got to her feet while wrapping my other arm around her waist.

Finally she would tell me she was okay and I would lead her to her bed. Lying on top of her blanket, she would speak of her love for me. Once again, she would tell me the story of the

December morning I was born, about how, the contractions beginning, she and my father raced for a taxi in Bergenfield and she fell into a snowdrift. You were almost born in the snow, she would say. Then she would close her eyes, and I would leave.

# 2

# SCREAMING FROM CARS

You can stand up for circumstances that hurt, outrage, or embarrass you because they are your circumstances. Even if you don't like yourself very much, or like where you come from, you will resent anyone who tells you that you and the place you come from are unacceptable. I was ashamed of my parents, I was enraged by them, but I was also protective of them. After Terry Calloway, a girl in my high school who was one of my father's piano students, suggested that my father was too shy to be a good teacher, I never spoke to her again. When from time to time kids mocked my mother's habit, both ingratiating and self-dramatizing, of calling people "sweetie" and "honey," I told them, in a rage of shame, to go fuck themselves.

The academically elite crowd at Paramus High School, who were mostly Jewish, brought out all my insecurities. They were composed. They were restrained. They rarely revealed what they were really thinking. In defiance of their composure, I turned my lack of inhibition into a type of pedigree.

In the cafeteria I would run around with the tray, begging the cafeteria workers for, say, beef Stroganoff in a Russian accent, or spaghetti with meatballs in an Italian accent. Or I would fall

to my knees before a beautiful girl and recite a parody of "How
Do I Love Thee?"

ME
How do I love thee? Let me count the ways. Let me see.
Number one: Your ears. Number two: Your fingers.
Number three: Your fingernails. Number four: Your
elbows. Number five: Your new Mustang. Number six—

GIRL
(*rolling her eyes*)
Let me know when you reach a million. (*She turns back
to her friends.*)

Or I would go up to Barry Goldberg and Barry Cohen, the two
leaders of the academically driven crowd, the first the class president, the second the vice president, and really let them have it:

ME
Hey! Uh-study your-uh salad hard, and turna inna
youra meatballs tomorrow onna time.

BARRY C
(*laughing good-naturedly but turning red*)
Okay, Lee.

ME
More Struuuuuuuganoff. More beeeeef Struuuuuuuganoff. I haff to eat to pleess my parents. To pleeeessss my
parents. Ya zig moy, vrog moy!

BARRY G
(*also blushing*)
Dasveedanya.

ME
I Italiano, not Russki. I-uh cook-uh you some braaaa-cheeeoli also. You-uh wanta some braaaacheeoli? Make-uh you strong. Make-uh you smart. Make-uh you get into Harvard.

BARRY G
(*the red in his face going from embarrassment to anger; but he still continues to laugh with a show of good nature*)
Yes, let's have some of that. That sounds good.

BARRY C
I love Italian food.

ME
I-uh love to eatta some pizza. Then to eatta some spa-ghetti. Then to eatta some cannoli. Then to-uh sit down, read some Aristotle—anda masturbate! Do you-uh like to masturbate?

(*Barry G and Barry C look at each other with shared an-noyance, then at the small crowd of other students who are laughing. They start to laugh.*)

ME
Your father, he-uh masturbates. You-uh canna be sure of thatta. Plato loved to masturbate, too. That's how he came up with his ideal forms. While he was jerking off.

(*Barry G and Barry C finish off their milk and pile their empty plates and cups neatly on their trays. They stand up.*)

BARRY C
Pardon me if I don't shake your hand, Mr. Plato.

**BARRY G**
We're off to class. Buon giorno, Signor Aristotle.

**ME**
Aristotle said that money fucks and makes interest the way parents make children. Don't forget!

**BARRY G AND BARRY C**
(*together*)
Ciao!

Self-suppression was not for me. I scorned people who didn't live for the gratifications of the moment. I saw them as conformists, people cowed by convention who spent their young lives in debt to some unknown future. I owed it to myself to enjoy the present. Any obligations to the future I would satisfy when the future arrived.

I found myself in a different group from the Jewish crowd, most of whose fathers were lawyers, doctors, architects, reasonably successful businessmen. My friends' fathers were electricians, cops, garbagemen, commercial artists, mailmen, pharmacists, insurance agents, cabdrivers. Matthew Cassidy was an exception. He awed us with tales of his father, Donald, who was an architect in New York. Sometimes I would stand with Matthew on the overpass above Route 17 and he would identify the buildings in the New York City skyline that he said his father had designed. The buildings were so far away that I could never make them out. Matthew explained that he had been to the city himself to see them so he knew exactly where they were.

Some boys I felt drawn to but never became friends with, like Joey Navas, whose father was a maintenance supervisor for the Port Authority. Joey was part of a group of tough kids who were of either Irish or Italian descent. Only one or two of them were real bullies, but once they started pushing people around, that became the group's hallmark and its criterion for cool.

Slowly, maybe without them even being aware of their transformation, the boys in the group went from being loud, funny, and daring to brutish and aggressive. I think that very few of them thought of themselves as bullies. Because an ego-gratifying sense of well-being flowed through them when they were pushing other people around, they felt that bullying was some special kind of virtue.

Joey was part of their crowd, but he never laid a hand on anyone. The other boys in his group treated him with respect, all the more because, not being outwardly clever, he was too inhibited to talk much. His silence, combined with his self-possession and sweet nature, gave him a certain authority. For me he seemed to have a particular solicitude. I don't know why. The one time his group came for me in a distant corner of the school's playing fields, Joey stepped between us and said, Leave him alone. He's a friend. Then he looked at me, his confidence with his group suddenly becoming shyness with me. He nodded to me and I nodded back as he sidled away to his crowd. We weren't really friends, and we never had anything to talk about.

After high school Joey became a plumber. Then he joined the New York and New Jersey Port Authority police. He had three children, and I found out later that he would bring their lunches to them in school on his days off in order to be closer to them and to delight them. One day in September, nearly thirty years after he had protected me in high school, he led a group of PA cops into a burning tower to try to save some strangers and never came out.

Is that what a very wealthy and very cultivated writer friend of mine meant when she once described someone as being "almost pathologically kindhearted"? Her phrase, set beside Joey's un-fathomable, militant kindness, has always agitated and perplexed me. If a person's kindness causes his destruction, then wouldn't the pathology be on the other side?

Sons of the lower middle class that we were, even in our extremest behavior my friends and I found ourselves, without meaning to, adhering to the law of moderation. We obstructed ourselves in distracted ways, but we were not not grimly self-thwarting; we were reckless, but not determined to die; indolent when it came to following the rules, but not delinquent.

We were earnest, too. When not too shy to speak at all—my aggressive antics were covers for my essential shyness—we often blurted out what we were really thinking. To compensate for our lack of well-heeled sophistication, we dressed with excessive formality whenever we went on a date.

On those occasions we discarded our usual torn sweaters or fraying knit shirts and dirty jeans in favor of permanent-press dress shirts. But these could not hide our awkwardness. In London once, a British book editor from the working class told me how in England, people quickly sum up your class origins and award or subtract "points" for your various mannerisms.

How about talking with your hands? I asked him.

Oh, he said, with a rich laugh, you lose a lot of points for that.

We could not resist using our hands when we talked. From a distance we must have looked like sailors shipwrecked on a deserted island, signaling to passing aircraft.

A famous magazine cover portrays the average New Yorker's mental map of the world as consisting of a vast foreground that is Manhattan, after which appears a small rectangle representing the country beyond, followed by the barely visible rest of the world.

If you had excavated the minds of my parents and my friends' parents, you would have found a map of the world in the form of a giant kitchen table. In the middle of its Formica surface sat an enormous pile of bills and small savings-account books with vinyl covers. The pile represented their lives in northern New Jersey. Pushed to the edge of the table, the salt and pepper shakers and napkin holder stood for the rest of the country, and the rest of the world. Budgetary conclaves around the kitchen table were weekly, sometimes nightly rituals for our parents.

The reality of need behind everyday appearance became imprinted on us. Teddy Di Buono's mailman father got him a summer job driving a mail truck and Teddy was caught by another mail carrier cutting pictures out of a *Playboy* magazine he was supposed to have been delivering. (He did this, he explained, as a protest against the pornography industry.) Teddy told us how the postal service supervisor threatened to fire his father as a result of his breach. He had heard his father on the phone begging a friend in the post office to intercede for him. Teddy related this story to us with wide-eyed horror.

We revolted against virtuous appearances that never acknowledged the struggle for survival behind them. This meant that we set ourselves against anyone who did not seem to be suffering or struggling.

We worked up our own type of social distinctiveness, out of which we tried to draw enough confidence to keep going. In this epic project, cars were indispensable.

We used to drink ourselves into near stupors while driving around town and listening to Led Zeppelin or Jethro Tull (if Paul Dolcetto or Peter Camino was driving), or Larry Coryell or Al Di Meola (if Tarmanian or Di Buono was driving), or Erroll Garner or Oscar Peterson (if I was behind the wheel). Camino liked to accelerate to eighty or ninety in an empty parking lot, slam on his brakes, and put the car into wild spins, during which we would hoot and cheer, too numb from alcohol to be frightened when the car was about to tip over. Paul simply drove as fast as he could, even when sober, all the while glancing distractedly out the window. On a highway once, with me in the passenger seat, he drove into the back of a school bus while looking at a snowy egret standing on the island between the highway's two directions. His head bounced off the steering wheel and into the windshield, leaving a cobweb of shattered glass. I hit the dashboard and escaped with a contusion on my forehead. His brain swelled and he was in the hospital for several days.

"Savage, extreme, rude, cruel, not to trust!" I would shout as with one friend or another we slowed the car down and passed the Beautiful Girl and Her Friends. It was a line that I memorized from a poem I had come across in my wanderings through the school library. I could not make heads or tails of the poem, but the words fit my antisocial impulses nicely. They also referred to despicable qualities that I believed respectable people hid within themselves.

I had a special fondness for the poem's first lines, though I had no inkling of what they meant, either—"The expense of spirit in a waste of shame / Is lust in action." The lines contained three words that I thought best expressed my singular virtues— "spirit," "lust," "action"—and one word that never failed to draw my attention: "shame." The girls would sometimes smile, and sometimes look annoyed.


Not long after the sheriff paid his visit to our house, four of us, so drunk that we had to take turns at the wheel, drove by the Paramus Police Department at night, shouting, "Dostoyevsky!

Dostoyevsky!" My friends, who were, like me, bookish yet not academic, thought the Russian name presented a strong anarchic statement. I had in mind Dostoyevsky's notion, in one of his tales, that the illogic of two plus two equals five was more truthful to human existence than the constructions of rational thought. Rational thinking was too compromised by considerations of survival and prosperity. I was also enamored of this line from the same book: "Lucidity is a great disease." The idea that clear thinking was a deficiency of character meant a lot to me.

Books provided a complete, self-sufficient alternative world. In this world, the gloom of economic misery that had driven happiness from my house was itself dispelled by new reference points, new parameters. The old stories, and the old ideas, usurped what I felt was money's supremacy. Even when a work of fiction—or play, or poem, or philosophical essay—was about money, money surrendered its status as being the abstract of everything. My cherished books themselves were about everything. Money was just one element of existence alongside all the others.

Money never had the last word in these books, even when money was the determining influence in a plot, or the central idea in a philosophical argument. The perspective from which the plot or argument was shaped occupied a plane above money. Rather than portraying money as gravely consequential, this higher perspective demonstrated the absurdity or inhumanity or at least insufficiency of a social arrangement in which money had such grave consequences.

My friends and I would often begin our drunken drives by smoking pot in someone's car in an empty parking lot. Later, we would buy a few six-packs of beer and move to another parking lot to finish those. After that we would drive around shouting our tokens of superiority, then gradually calm down and fall into long conversations about the meaning of life, and so forth. We often ended the night back in one of the original parking lots. There we vowed eternal allegiance to each other before parting.

One night, when we had dispensed with the pot-smoking prelude and sat thoughtfully drinking beer in Alex Tarmanian's light green Toyota in the parking lot of a bank, an orange Ford Pinto pulled up beside us. We often roamed through the night in a caravan of two or three cars when there were a few of us, so it was not unusual to be joined by someone in another car.

Tonight it was me, Paul, and two other friends: Peter Camino, a Puerto Rican kid who was the only person in town from what we used to call a "minority" background, though his father was a modestly successful commercial artist in New York; and Arthur Teitelbaum, whose father had patented a new and better machine for stringing tennis rackets, an invention that had propelled the Teitelbaums into the solid middle of the middle class.

Arthur was my only Jewish friend, besides Terry Cushman, though I was closer to Arthur. Terry never laughed at my jokes until other people did. It seemed to me that he laughed with a touch of hostility, as if he resented having to satisfy the emotional need that lay beneath my comic capering.

Arthur looked sad and dreamy most of the time. As soon as someone made a joke, he burst into easy laughter. Then he would abruptly look sad and dreamy again. He really belonged with the Goldbergs and the Cohens, but he fell in with us because he did not excel academically. He felt more comfortable with kids who pretended to laugh their shortcomings away. It was our laughter and lack of conscientiousness, however, that seemed to make him sad, since what he really wanted was to be with the Goldbergs and the Cohens.

The boy behind the wheel of the Pinto was not Jewish or Puerto Rican or ethnic at all. His name was John Linville. His father, Michael, was a prominent architect in town. Michael also served as one of the leaders of the Paramus Rotary Club, which numbered among its members various local politicians and zoning officials. Because of his success as an architect, and his eminence as a Rotarian, he stood at the convergence of wealthy clients and town officials who could be useful in the awarding of bids to developers and contractors—who in turn might be useful in bringing a realtor on board at the right time.

My father was courting Michael Linville in hopes of being invited into the Rotary Club. One day, when I was fourteen or fifteen, he came home beaming with excitement. Linville, he proudly informed us, had asked him to join the Rotary Club on a trip to the Army-Navy football game, which was to be played in Philadelphia. To my ambivalent delight—he embarrassed me; I wanted to see the legendary game—my father asked me if I would like to go with him.

Monroe was as far from WASP decorum as Jupiter is from Mars. Sitting next to my father on the bus that had been chartered by the Rotarians, I listened as he mentioned to Michael Linville something about some property somewhere. Linville commented on the Army quarterback. My father countered with a reference to another property. Linville commented on the Navy quarterback. Not one to be outdone, my father raised the subject of a beautiful commercial space that he had seen in Hackensack from the window of the Electra, and Linville smiled. He turned away to speak to his wife.

A couple of weeks later, my father returned from work ashen-faced. Following a wordless dinner, he vanished into the den, where he listened to jazz and ate cookies for hours before going to bed. I later heard my mother telling Judy Baum on the phone that he had been turned down by the Rotary Club, after all. For this reason, I both hated John Linville and longed to be accepted by him.

The straw-haired Linville had tiny yellow pinwheels embedded in his hazel eyes. He squinted behind wire-framed glasses. Rolling down the window of his Ford Pinto, he asked us what we were up to. He reached beside him and held up a six-pack of Heineken. This was, at the time, an exotic import that reduced our Budweisers and Michelobs to drab old standbys. He nodded to me and I immediately nodded back.

Hey, he said, nodding to me again. Ride with me.

Do you mind? I asked my friends, though I looked at Paul when I said it.

We'll be right behind you, Camino said.

It's strictly business, said Teitelbaum, echoing the line from *The Godfather*, which made absolutely no sense in the context. He laughed. Then he gazed sadly out the window.

Good stuff, said Paul. He patted my arm as I got out of the car.

Linville nodded to me again as I settled into the passenger seat next to him. When Paul and the others started to move, he began to slowly follow them. As they drove out of the parking lot onto the road that ran behind it, he sped up and raced toward Route 17, at the opposite end of the lot.

Where are you going? I said.

He held up a bottle of beer. Have one, he said. He pointed with the bottle to the glove compartment. The opener's in there, he said. He steered the trundling Pinto out onto the shoulder, pressed his foot to the accelerator, and we whipped onto the highway.

•

Route 17 ran, as I have said, north up into New York state, and south toward New York City, where it ended at the George Washington Bridge. Its stretch in Paramus was thick with furniture stores, shoe stores, car dealerships, diners, pizzerias, and other businesses. During the day and early evening, the highway was crowded with commuters and shoppers. On a Saturday night like the one with Linville, the highway gradually, as the night wore on, gave way, in some survival of the fittest in reverse, to drivers who were less and less sober. Accidents were common late at night, and also during rush hour, when merging onto or off the shoulder made you a sitting duck for cars performing the same operation.

Until recently, Route 17 had claimed its share of pedestrians, too. Kids dashed across the six-lane highway out of impulse, or on a dare. They would cross the three lanes of traffic going in one direction, stop in the narrow strip in the middle, wait for their chance, and race over the final three lanes.

For this reason, Route 17, as well as its east-west twin, Route 4, haunted the parents of Paramus. They warned their children, on pain of harsh punishment, to stay away from the highways. They begged for action from town officials, who in turn appealed to the state. But because of the expense of putting up a barrier between directions, plus the lack of a financial incentive for any New Jersey politician to take on the bureaucracy to implement the plan, the pleas came to nothing. Every once in a while the monster highways devoured another victim. It was chilling to see, on a dark Halloween night, children dressed as ghosts and skeletons trick-or-treating along the shoulder of Route 17 or Route 4.

The menace began to be brought under some kind of control when I was in junior high. As if in some macabre sacrifice, a teenage girl rushed across Route 17 to be with her friends as they stood waving and beckoning to her on the other side. A car hit her without braking, at seventy miles per hour. The impact had so much force that, as her friends watched, her separated leg spun up into the air over the traffic.

Weeks later, money was found to begin construction on a concrete wall, two and a half feet high, that would divide Route 17's two directions. A year or two after that, and about five decades since Route 17 was inaugurated as a major highway, during which time countless people died on it, various local politicians and zoning officials took credit for what was touted as the life-saving measure of the divider.

But the long, shallow wall had the effect of, literally, raising the bar for some kids. Now it served as a coveted marker. The ultimate gamble became to race to the divider and sit, straddling it, shouting and whooping in triumph, before scrambling across the final three lanes to the other side. Kids still died. Parents still lay awake at night, confused by their inability to guarantee the welfare of their children in a place they had moved to in order to be safe. My friends and I would never have dreamed of setting foot on either of the highways. Depending on how you looked at it, crossing them was either an advanced rite of passage for people who had the inborn confidence to take their future for granted, or a destructive test of courage for people who refused to accept their essential fearfulness.

John Linville was picking up speed, squinting harder at the streaming night-lights of the cars, stores, and streetlamps. He turned on the radio. Captain and Tenille's "Love Will Keep Us Together" was playing. He turned it up, singing at the top of his lungs.

Cars had two seat belts for each person back then. I buckled the one around my waist, then pulled the sash around my shoulder and locked it into its clasp.

Don't you trust me? said Linville.

I saw that he had not buckled either of his seat belts.

For a moment I thought of undoing mine, but the cat was already out of the bag. I was obviously scared. Demonstrating that I wasn't would have made me look scared twice. I shrugged and laughed. I wanted to show that I at least had the courage not to care about appearing frightened.

How about some jazz? I said, reaching for the radio.

Linville pushed my hand away. I hate jazz, he said with a smile.

Swaying back and forth behind the wheel, he continued to sing along with the radio. The car began to sway, too. I looked at the odometer. We were going almost sixty-five.

Gliding into the middle lane, Linville placed his hand on the gear selector and moved the car into second gear. Since the car had an automatic transmission, there was no reason to do this, and downshifting made no sense anyway, but we all drove cars with automatic transmissions, and we all liked to pretend that we were driving a stick. Focusing on this driving make-believe, Linville had stopped veering to the left and right. I relaxed a little and spoke to him with gratitude.

Cool car, I said.

Yeah, he said. My dad bought it for me last year. Pintos are very cool, he said.

Tony Orlando and Dawn's "He Don't Love You (Like I Love You)" came on. Linville started to sing loudly again. He jerked the car left to right as he swayed back and forth. I tried to recall some of my favorite jazz songs, "Autumn Leaves" or "Poinciana," to calm myself. The terrific speed of the car reduced the tunes in my head to a silly irrelevancy.

This car really moves, I said.

Yeah, he said. Watch this. Shifting senselessly from drive into second again, and then back into drive, he moved into the fast lane. Now we were moving at about seventy-five.

Whoa, I said.

Yes! he cried. He took a swig of his beer. Then he pressed the brake pedal, slowed the car down, and swerved into the concrete divider. The Pinto bounced off it, shook and vibrated like crazy, and stabilized.

Yeah!! he screamed. I began to yell in fright, but fear of seeming frightened overwhelmed my fear of being hurt or dying, and my yell came out as a wild hoot of complicity. Whooo-hooooo! I cried. Gulping down my beer, I pulled another one out of the carton and flipped off the top with the opener. Linville finished his beer, opened his window, and threw the bottle out of the car. I heard the popping and shattering glass grow fainter in the distance.

Fuck yeah! he yelled, and hit the divider again. I could see that he was pressing the brake as the car struck the divider, quickly taking his foot off on impact, then braking again. But the car shook and vibrated even more violently this time. For a moment Linville lost control.

Whoaaaaa! he cried. He wrestled the Pinto down and straightened it out.

That was a close one, I said.

Not as close as this, he said, hitting the divider. The Pinto bounced off it again, and again he struggled to straighten it out, breathing heavily and pushing his glasses up his nose after he did so. He turned to me. Fuuuuuuuck! he shouted, staring into my eyes while he steadied the car with the brake. Fuuuuuuuuuuck! he shouted again. He accelerated and struck the divider again and again. There was a maniacal fixity in his eyes. In the green and yellow reflected lights of the highway, he looked like a ghoul.

I stopped yelling. Summoning the Old Man, I described to myself what was happening, as if the world was watching and listening years later, when the night's events became a story. "The car is hitting the divider. Linville turned to look at me. I sat quietly, letting it happen. My eyes stung with anguish and anger. In the green light of the highway he looked like a ghoul." But the

Old Man couldn't help me that night. I felt all the more help-less for relying on him.

Tiring of hitting the divider, or feeling that he should not push his luck any further, Linville was now weaving in and out of traffic at about ninety.

I love this fucking car, he said. Don't you love this fuck-ing car?

It's a cool car, I said shakily. Linville peered over at me.

Maybe it's time to meet up with those guys, he said.

I nodded.

Where are they? he said. I had no idea. Up ahead I saw the Century movie theater, which sat near the intersection of Route 17 and Route 4.

They're there, I said. We always meet up in the parking lot over there.

Linville looked at me and smiled.

Sure, he said. We have to get you to your friends. Don't worry, we'll get you to your friends. Do you see them?

No, I said. But they'll be there. We arranged to meet there.

This was untrue. My friends and I had said nothing about meeting at the Century. But getting away from Linville was worth the price of the transparent lie. I felt desolate. The castle was a dreary split-level house, the Old Man had disappeared, and the jazz songs were not my songs.

Here you are, said Linville, stopping at the edge of the park-ing lot.

Thanks, I said as I got out of the car. Good stuff.

He smiled straight into my eyes, locking them into his. He did this for about thirty seconds. Then he drove off without saying a word. I could not see the side of the car that had struck the divider, but it must have been all banged up.

Standing alone at the edge of the parking lot, now deserted because of the late hour, I fought off the impulse to drop to my knees and kiss the crossroads of Route 4 and Route 17. There were too many Saturday-night revelers still passing by. I checked my watch. It was nearly three o'clock. Paul would be home by now. I decided to risk angering his mother and call him to ask if he could come get me. I walked along the highway in search of a pay phone.

Caught up in my escapades with my friends, and in my withdrawal into books, I was suffering in school. I might have been able to talk with relentless sincerity about Othello—whose bombast, meant by Shakespeare to reveal Othello's fatal flaws of insecurity and self-regard, I envied—but the outcome of this was that I grew alienated from subjects, like math and science, for which I had no flair. I had convinced myself that I was endowed with a unique connection to literature. As a result, I granted myself a reprieve from any type of academic work that brought me frustration rather than the pleasure literature afforded me.

I did much better in my English classes than in math and science. But Othello's formal diction didn't help me when it came to taking the standardized aptitude tests that colleges used to help determine your suitability. My performance on the verbal part of the exam was just respectable. My math scores were so low that I felt I had to go around and tell everyone how low they were in order to make light of them.

When the senior-year ritual of conferring about college with the high school guidance counselor came around, I should have presented a rich contradiction. Possessing a knack for language and for analytical reading, I was faltering in school. Devoted to books as living forms of experience, I performed without distinction on tests meant to measure my grasp of literature as a repository of sacred information. The contradiction, however, was in my eyes only. My teachers and school administrators looked at me as a touching fuckup and daydreamer, who required too much time and energy to be set straight.

But in my eyes, the lack of social recognition was a blessing. My integrity, the way I saw it, came to depend on my ability to keep my exceptional gifts away from the tawdry currents of the transactional world. Out there my gifts would be held under scrutiny, They would be compared with the actions and accomplishments of other, dissimilar people. So long as my gifts went unrecognized, they remained unchallenged. So long as I did not have to test them, I would never doubt their existence.


Mr. Crostini, the guidance counselor, stood up and came out from behind his desk to welcome me into his office. His gesture would have reassured me if he had not walked with such impatience. After showing me in, he held his door open as he leaned with his hand on the doorknob and said to the two or three other boys waiting to see him on plastic chairs outside his office: I'll just be a minute. As I passed by him, I smelled his breath. It was stale from the menthol cigarettes that he chain-smoked.

He sat behind his large wooden desk and lit another cigarette. Exhaling, he leaned back in his high leather chair with his hands joined behind his head. Since he was in his early forties, the lock of hair that fell over his forehead seemed less boyish and more a piece of his past that he had, with the same impatience, allowed to remain. He was wearing a light brown corduroy sport jacket that was starting to loosen and bulge from overuse.

He glanced at some papers in an open manila folder that lay before him. It was my dossier. He was not upbeat about my future. Though my English classes were in the A range, my grade point average was between a B and a C. It was unfortunate, he said matter-of-factly, that I did not seem very conscientious about school. He smiled to himself and shook his head.

I began to talk faster. To my surprise, I wanted him to know that I was more than the sum of the cold facts in my file. I wanted him to know that there was something more to me than the lackluster student who cut class occasionally, handed in unremarkable homework, and lacked enthusiasm for his classes. I became indignant about being reduced to what people thought they knew about me from the way I behaved; I wanted him to know that my true meaning lay in all the experiences I was going through; this, I believed, made my inner life more valuable than what mere grades proved—

Dear Mr. Crostini:

We met in your office forty years ago. I hope that you are still alive and, if you are, that you are as well as can be expected.

Forgive the delay in writing to you, but I would like to amplify the remarks I made to you that afternoon in 1975, in hopes of correcting a mistaken impression that you may have had of me.

You seem to have derived from what you believed were my laziness, irresponsibility, and insolent gestures a judgment of me as possessing average to below-average intelligence and creativity. But what you perceived as laziness and irresponsibility was, in reality, a paralysis of the will, induced by a lack of confidence, itself caused by a breakdown in parental authority, which in turn was the product of a confluence of characterological and circumstantial factors that might or might not have had the same unfortunate effects in a different social and economic arrangement.

My paralysis in school was actually the result of an

incredible number of projects that I was involved in outside the regular curriculum. If it is not too late, please add to my file these extramural activities, all of which consisted of my attempts to accumulate sufficient confidence to permit myself to accept a place in the always-room-for-one-more honeycomb of social relations:

- Driving recklessly and fast, which offered escape from a tempestuous home life, provided an efficient and, so long as I maintained control of the car, violence-free outlet for fantasies of power, compensated for a sense of inertia, and developed poise in stressful situations.

- Seeking out, in traditional heterosexual adolescent fashion, girls—a vital aspect of socialization that, in my case, acquired a particular urgency in light of my father's personal admission to me of his sexual impotence, and my mother's efforts to seduce me; please note that these efforts were unsuccessful.

- Drinking excessive and, in some cases, stupefying amounts of alcohol, a rigorously structured undertaking that moderated my anger, eased debilitating levels of tension, and enabled me, before vomiting or passing out, to envision myself in situations in which responsibility, piety, stability, selflessness, and self-respect constituted the hallmarks of my personality.

- Going to extreme lengths to entertain people and make them laugh: an exercise in masochism and self-hatred that indicated a commitment to public service, as well as demonstrating a desire to act beyond my own narrow self-interest.

In short, you misjudged me. I am well aware that this is a common error, not just in your line of endeavor but in many professions where time constraints and daunting logistics make the rapid and therefore incomplete appraisal of a person unavoidable. Then, too, who can see into someone's inner depths, or future?

Still, if I may say so, it is small misperceptions like these that can sometimes have the effect of preventing an individual from reaching his or her full potential. You yourself, had you perhaps been the beneficiary of a more nuanced approach as a youth, might have gone on, not to squander your distinctive skills in the role of high school guidance counselor responsible for steering in the right direction teenagers whose bold defiance was in inverse proportion to their lostness and meekness, but to reach your full potential as, for example, a bookkeeper for a drug cartel.

Thank you very much for your time. Please be assured that I harbor no hard feelings against you. Decades of experience have taught me that we do the best we can with what we are given. I hope you have a wonderful day.

Sincerely,

Mr. Crostini closed my folder and stood up. Apply to William Paterson, he said. You have a good chance of getting in. Stretching out his hand over his desk, he wished me luck.


Located in the white, lower-middle-class suburb of Wayne, New Jersey, William Paterson College was a state college known as a school for jocks and for kids who wanted to enter trades like construction and landscaping. In an earlier time, they would not have needed a college degree to pursue the work they wanted, or had to settle for. Nearly all the students desired jobs in some corner of commerce, or on the lower slopes of finance.

What I expected from college was not available at William Paterson. My mother had gone to Hunter and my father never went to college. I believed I deserved better. To my mind, my intimate connection to books and my grades in English proved it. After my boredom in high school, and the commotion at home, I wanted college to be a transformative experience. Even the kids from modest economic backgrounds like mine put together enough loans and financial aid to attend a good private college. Paul was going to Drew University in Madison, though staying in New Jersey, close to my parents, was out of the question. I wanted an elevated intellectual adventure and complete emotional independence. After being in Mr. Crostini's office, I was no longer content to thrive in secret.

I sent away to William Paterson for its catalogs anyway. I would segue from one passionate certitude to another, and my certainty that Crostini was underestimating me quickly gave way to my certainty that he was looking out for my best interests.

The tired categories high school imposed on even the most exciting subjects numbed me. By contrast, the idea of an entire semester devoted to a subject in philosophy or literature seemed the embodiment of the freedom I had been seeking. The very facts of a "semester" and of the complete immersion into a single area of culture made higher education seem like an end in itself.

But that was not what I found, devouring the catalogs as if they were prospectuses of an afterlife. The courses were few, and superficial. Subjects I prized, such as philosophy, were barely represented. There was a great emphasis on fulfilling requirements, graduating, and getting out.

Worst of all, Paterson was a commuter school. That meant that I would not have the four years I had been counting on as

an Elysian break in the speeding space-time continuum of one
worldly obligation after another. College, for me, had nothing
to do with laying the groundwork for a career. I didn't see it as
the next stage in the evolution of a life. I considered it nothing
less than a salvation.

I rejected William Paterson as a possibility, and also other
state schools, such as Montclair, Glassboro, and Ramapo. Rutgers,
New Jersey's premier state university, seemed like a place that
might fulfill my expectations of enlightenment and expanded
meaningfulness. But it was too close to home.

My mother didn't want me staying in New Jersey, either. She
was planning to divorce my father. After that, she expected
Angelo to come live with her. Since he would be bringing along
his three children, and my brother was still in junior high, there
would be no space for me. Shedding a few tears of self-sacrifice,
my mother had already told me that I was free to take my beloved
Ethan Allen desk, chair, and hutch with me to whatever college
I chose, so long as I could find the money to transport them.

My living nearby but in a dormitory, or in a room off campus, was also not palatable to her. We fought all the time. The
mere sight of me seemed to provoke in her unfulfilled longings,
or past resentments, or unfinished business with my father. In
college she saw a legitimate opportunity to send me away. She
appeased her conscience by reassuring me that a state school was
beneath my gifts.

My father joined in urging me to attend a distant school. He
was living in a rented room in a private home in a nearby town.
Somehow he had managed to find another job in real estate.
Sobered up for the moment by events, robbed of the marriage
and the home that had permitted him to fantasize about a future
that was rapidly slipping away from him, he did not want me
to see him flailing in his reduced circumstances.

He did not have to worry about that. I refused to visit him in his room because I knew that seeing him there would have crushed me.

My parents could not afford to pay for my college education. My mother had been unable to find a position as a full-time teacher. She was getting by on a combination of her income as a substitute and the money my father was sending her as stipulated by their divorce settlement. My father's new job at a real estate firm paid a rudimentary salary—no draw this time—and seemed to be, from what my mother told me, a temporary situation. After the money he sent my mother, he had just enough left over to satisfy his own needs.

Since even the tuition at a state university would have been beyond their means, my parents were indifferent to whether I attended a public or a private school. They were too distracted by their own more urgent predicaments. They automatically assumed that I would fulfill their middle-class expectation that their children would go on to four years of higher education. My mother, the child of immigrants, and my father, the product of a household driven into economic despair by the death of his own father, regarded college for their sons to be as much a staple of their existence as a car—though my mother would soon change her tune about that, as about so many things. Thanks to student loans and financial aid, a private college that was a few thousand dollars a year more than a state school was within reach. I would simply have to take out more loans for a private college. And a private college was what I wanted. I did not want college to be a perfunctory step forward.

In those pre-Internet days, I sent away to about a dozen of the most affordable liberal arts colleges for catalogs. Bradley University in Peoria, Illinois, came closest to satisfying my expectations. It was almost one thousand miles away, for one thing.

For another, the midwestern school offered one of the few undergraduate degrees in journalism. My passion for words, my desire to use them as levers to change my place in the world, and a TV show about heroic magazine writers called *The Name of the Game* had made me resolve to become a journalist. Most important of all, considering my checkered performance in high school, Bradley had one of the highest acceptance rates among small private colleges.

It never occurred to me that visiting the college was a necessary step for seriously considering it. The idea of travel was too remote for that to be an option. Neither of my parents had the money to afford to fly to Peoria with me. Both of them were too depressed to drive with me there, or to take me to Bradley in some other, less expensive way. Even if they had mustered enough spirit to do so, my father was too nervous about losing another job to take any time off, and my mother could not afford to miss too many days of teaching. As for me, I was as unconcerned about a practical convention like exploring the university where you were thinking of spending the next four years of your life as I was about the basic facts of science. If I had been told that Peoria was in a different time zone, I would have been surprised to hear it.

The day Bradley's letter of acceptance arrived, I was stunned. It was the first time that something of great worth, something that I had imagined embracing me, became a reality.

The one catch was, as my mother reminded me, that I would have to work my way through school. But this didn't faze me. I had been exchanging labor for money since I was a child.

### *"The Tale of the Four Quarters"*

My best friend, Matthew Cassidy, and I arrived at the Adlers' with rakes in hand. We had come straight from Stony Lane elementary school, walking along a small wooden bridge over a shallow stream. A crossing guard wearing a blue uniform with gold buttons shepherded us across a busy avenue. She snapped at anyone who lingered as they crossed or stopped to say hello to her. A short, mild, introspective boy, Matthew was a Beatles fan. He sang their songs softly to himself as we walked ("I'll buy you a diamond ring my friend / If it makes you feel all right . . .").

We reached the Adlers' yard. There were dead and dying leaves everywhere. They were brilliant and beautiful, but they were rotting. We could smell their decaying sweetness as we worked. Our job was to rake the leaves into piles and then to press the piles with our hands into large black plastic bags. After that, we had to leave the bags on the curb in front of the Adlers' light blue split-level house. The garbage truck would come and take them away to be incinerated.

On our way to the Adlers', we passed Matthew's house. Painted a rustic red, the tiny cottage sat just across the street from the bridge as we walked off it. The red cottage was full of the sound of laughter and the smell of good food. Matthew's father, Donald, a short Irishman with damp, laughing eyes, had grown up in the city, in Hell's Kitchen. Violet, his mother, was a large Italian American woman who spent the morning watching television and cooked in a happy trance during the afternoon. Matthew loved them, and they loved him.

Matthew, his parents, and his sister, Kathy, were Catholic. They were initiates, as Matthew recounted to me, in the mysteries of confession, where horrendous sins were forgiven in a cadence of ancient words. I was drawn in a spell of fascination to this idea of mercy triumphing over justice. In the rite of communion, Matthew said, the hammered and battered body of Christ became transformed into white wafers and red wine. Mercy and the healing of wounded matter seemed to me to be at the magical heart of Matthew's religion.

On top of that mystery was another one: Matthew's father took the bus every morning from Paramus to New York, where he worked in the silver-spired Empire State Building. His face glowing, Matthew boasted to me about his father's accomplishments as an architect. He was responsible for several skyscrapers in the city, Matthew explained, glowing and blushing. Matthew would sometimes draw the tall buildings for me in his gold-spiraled notebook when we were in school.

Originally a collection of celery farms, Paramus began to flourish after the Second World War. Lying only seventeen miles from New York City, it offered an ideal commute, especially to veterans returning from Europe and Japan in triumph, and then from Korea. Those who were not too shattered to begin a promising new life could afford Paramus's modest tract houses with the help of the GI Bill. That was how my father, a veteran of the Korean War, came to buy our split-level house in 1961.

Many of the town's residents worked in the shopping malls and in the stores that lined the highways. I found positions as a stock boy and then a salesman in the department stores. That was where I worked part-time during my last two years of high school. My first real job was as a stock boy at Alexander's, a giant department store on Route 4 that catered to low-income people who mostly visited from the poorer sections of New York City. If they had the money for the commute, they could purchase attractive clothes of inferior quality.

The store sported a mural, at the time perhaps the largest public mural in the world, on its facade. A Polish artist named Stefan Knapp, who was sent to a Siberian gulag as a young man in Poland after Stalin's agents murdered his father, had been commissioned by the store's owner, George Farkas, to paint it.

In the Soviet prison colony Knapp nearly starved to death. After being released from the gulag, as a result of an agreement between Poland and the Soviet Union, he fought in the RAF. He stayed in London after the war. Eventually he took up painting public murals. He flourished and became something of a celebrity. *Life* magazine did a spread on him, using photographs of him constructing the Alexander's mural. He slid on skis from one end of the giant mural to another. In the photographs, he looks cheerful and robust.

Farkas, an admirer and collector of modernist painting, had envisioned a work of art that would please rich and poor, educated and uneducated, sophisticated people and people with simple tastes. But the finished product, a giant rectangular painting that appeared on the front of the store in 1962, did not have the universal appeal Farkas had hoped for.

To some people, the masses of primary colors resembled an uplifting map of the world, in which the familiar continents existed in a harmony of form and content. To others, the mural was a horrifying mess about to liquefy and collapse into sheets of multicolored lava that would crush the crowds of people below with vicious force. The residents of Paramus sat around their kitchen tables arguing about whether, in an ideal situation, the town authorities should allow the mural to remain or remove it on the pretext that the eyesore repelled people passing through town who otherwise might have stopped and visited the stores.

That late autumn afternoon, Matthew and I finished our work just as it was growing dark. We rang the bell. Mrs. Adler, wearing loose slacks and her husband's slippers, came to the door. She dropped four bright shiny quarters into each of our hands with a kind, weak smile. I did not understand why she was wearing her husband's slippers. I said goodbye to Matthew and ran home, clutching the coins in my hand. I had no idea what they meant, or why I had received four rather than one, two, or twenty. But I felt proud and excited.

I carried them to my mother, who cooed with happiness

and stroked my face. She took me upstairs to her bedroom. Opening a drawer, she lifted out a jewelry box that I had made for her in school by gluing dried macaroni to the top of a cigar box and spray-painting the whole thing gold.

We both sat on the edge of the bed. I put the coins in her hand. She sat there with the change in her hand and said, "This is the first money you earned yourself, my darling boy. I am going to keep this money here, in the box you made for me. It will always be there for you. When you are older and all grown up, it will still be here, waiting for you." Holding a coin up, she showed me the distinguished likeness on its front. Then she put the change in the box and placed the box back in the drawer. She kissed me on my cheek.

A few years later, after the situation at home had changed, my mother told me that Shelly Adler was a fraud who had lied about a relationship with my father so that he could ingratiate himself with a developer whom he was trying to convince to collaborate with him on a luxury apartment complex. She also said that Matthew Cassidy's father was an alcoholic who worked as an office boy for an architectural firm. The Adlers' small, run-down split-level house with its tiny yard has been bought and sold many times since then, but it is still there. The jewelry box disappeared decades ago. I don't know if any of the quarters remain in circulation, or if they were all withdrawn, melted down, and turned into brand-new coins.

I can't recall where or when I read an essay about adventure that has stuck in my mind ever since. Adventure was, in this account, a break in the cause and effect that rules our lives. It was an independent, self-sufficient piece of experience that had its own dynamic, its own laws, its own beginning, middle, and end. The experience of adventure resembled a work of art.

I liked this line in the essay especially: the adventurer "is not determined by any past, nor, on the other hand, does the future exist for him."

I grew up as a mall adventurer. My friends and I played games of tag in Paramus's malls from the time we were old enough to take the bus to the Garden State Plaza and the Bergen Mall. One person closed his eyes and counted. Everyone else would disperse among the racks, bins, mirrors, and fitting rooms, nearly knocking customers down, and fleeing from the store security.

I didn't consider the stores places of crass commercialism. I saw them as instances of transubstantiation, like Matthew Cassidy's mysterious sacraments: realms of retail freedom.

On display, for sale, belonging to some abstract company only as long as no one purchased them, the objects in these stores were pure, deracinated forms: sovereign and autonomous— mirror images of my ideal self. They were material things that had been liberated from matter and transported into my imagination. Playing among them, I could release myself from the facts of my life that weighed me down.

In the furniture department, I was a husband and father, returning home to the solid possessions of sofa, armchair, bureau, wardrobe, all of them so heavy and established on the floor that no upheaval could move them. I was in a state of joy when I hid behind a dresser so big that none of my friends could see me. In men's furnishings, as I concealed myself behind racks of clothes, I could imagine myself as a secret agent or an architect in a dark blue suit.

Women's clothing had its allure, too. My friends and I might have sworn allegiance time and again, in one bewildered male-bonding rite after another, to the romantic pursuit of girls, but it delighted me to disappear into a fitting room and slip into a summer dress or a miniskirt. Fur coats sent me over the moon.

Once I tried one on, fascinated by the first split second in which I failed to recognize myself.

As I became more alienated at home and in school, the alienating environment of the department stores grew more comforting. In Alexander's, where I started as a stock boy, I worked alongside mostly black kids and young black men from Paterson, Newark, and nearby Ridgewood, the last an affluent white town with a sizable population of poor black people. We carried boxes of clothes out to the floor, where we refilled the vast bins with them. There was the usual basic solidarity in work, but because they were black, and I was white, relations between us were self-conscious even as we pretended that the differences did not exist. We were considerate to each other where we might have been casually helpful. This created an actual, if temporary, bond where there would otherwise have been merely a working relationship. But the bond was deliberate. Sometimes it fell into place, and sometimes it was strenuous—and sometimes the other person or I wanted no part of any bond at all. Wherever a bond existed, though, whether it was comfortable or labored at, we had to construct it from scratch each time we found ourselves working together.

Boy, you are quite the worker bee, a slender black guy with delicate hands that reminded me of my father's said to me one evening. His friends laughed as I pushed myself to stack one fresh box of clothes after another on the shelves in the stockroom. He winked to his friends and put his arm around my shoulders. Take a break, he said.

I sat down on a box, wiping my forehead with my sleeve. He and his friends finished unloading my cart. They stacked everything neatly on the shelves, side by side. Time's a feather when you work together, he intoned, deepening his voice and glancing over at the others. A few bent their heads, chuckling. He clapped me gently on my back.

Many of the saleswomen were also black. To my surprise, some of them returned my interest in them. Whereas the white girls my age flirted in indirect code-language and through evasive gestures, the black girls addressed me sincerely and with a kind of motherly warmth. No matter how sensual they appeared to me, and how much they flirted, they all seemed to me to have this maternal warmth way at the back of their sensuality. It was especially strong, to the point where the flirtatiousness disappeared, in the presence of the black guys who worked with me in the stockroom.

There was an anthropological quality to the women's interest in me, too. They knew all about turbulence and anguish, but I don't think very many of them had encountered that state in an approachable, sympathetic-seeming white boy, and at such close quarters. From time to time, I had to go somewhere and sit staring into space. They considered me with curiosity and sympathy.

For my part, I regarded them with guarded expectation. We shared a lot of jokes. The humor dissolved the preexisting unease between us and created a new, pleasurable tension. Together we moved around inside the same half-playful, half-experimental bubble. At the end of every shift we said goodbye with smiles of complicity, as if to congratulate each other on completing that day's or night's two activities: straightforward work and a kind of confused, excited pretense—electric with promise but signifying and leading to nothing.


Walking into one of the great department stores was like entering another universe. Bamberger's, Gimbels, Stern's, Alexander's: in my eyes, they embodied mysteries, like the pyramids. I worked three evenings a week after school, and also on Saturdays. I made roughly eighty dollars per week, and every Friday night I gave my mother something like thirty or forty dollars.

Of course there were the long stretches of time deadened by rote work, stretches during which you would glance at your watch, see that it was five after seven, help some customers, straighten some racks, take instructions from one of your bosses, and look at your watch again after all that time-consuming activity, only to see that it was seven-ten.

But I could dress up! I could transform myself in preparation for that shift's transformations. The telltale formality of the permanent-press shirts I wore on dates, which made me feel awkward even as I submitted to the habit of wearing them, didn't matter in the store. Everyone who worked there, including the stock boys, dressed formally, as if for church. I wore a crisp oxford shirt and a pair of dress pants with an ineradicable crease.

Roaming in your best clothes through the department you had been assigned to, you felt how the parameters of existence had changed. The people who approached you, or to whom you offered assistance, played a strange new role: they were customers. You were the salesman. And they needed you. Given my prim aversion to any type of human interaction defined by financial terms, I should have deplored the empty transactionality of it all. Instead I prized the elemental purity in the relationship between salesman and customer.

All life revolves around what people want. There would be no history and no culture if people did not want things, and if different people did not want different things. Underneath the layer upon layer of social convention and psychological defense, there is always the naked fact of wanting. "Can I help you?" "Yes, I am looking for a vest." "What type of vest?" "A white vest that I can wear under a dark sport coat." "What size are you?" "I wear a forty-six." "Why don't you try this? Here you go." "Thank you." "You're very welcome. How does it fit?" "It's a little snug."

"Yes, I see. Why don't you try this?" "Thank you." "You're very welcome. How does that fit?" "I like it." "Yes?" "Yes, I do. Do you have it in yellow?" "Yellow?" "Yes, I think I'd prefer it in yellow." "No, I'm sorry. It comes in black and beige." "You like it in beige?" "Absolutely." "I don't look fat?" "Not at all." "It's not too loose down here?" "No. But if it feels loose, you can always do that. Or that. There you go." "It doesn't bulge up here?" "No." "Okay, then. I'll take it." "Wonderful." "Where do I pay?" "Right up there. Turn left at the end of that aisle." "That way?" "No, this way." "This way?" "No, that way. Yes. And then turn left." "Thank you." "No, to the left." "Thank you." "You're very welcome."

Outside the store, Charles Manson was serving time for recently slicing up the pregnant Sharon Tate and her friends. Vietnam was being seared with napalm. The genocidal Khmer Rouge was coming to power. Nixon's henchmen had broken into the Watergate Hotel. My mother was waiting at home for me in her new tight jeans, and my father was staring out the window in his rented room. In the world outside, the square pegs and round holes of perversely or savagely misaligned desires led to pain and misery. The department stores, however, had rationalized desire down to a science. In them, you were not afraid to be troubled, damaged, defeated, or dead.

I did some research and discovered a department store in downtown Peoria called Bergner's. I planned to apply for a job there once I settled in at Bradley.

Not long after I received the acceptance letter from Bradley, and after my brother had gone to sleep, my mother and I sat at the kitchen table, going over the budget for college. My mother's voice broke as we talked about my living nearly a thousand miles away from her. Yet as the fact of the freedom that awaited me stared us both in the face, her eyes contracted with that envy

that still confounded me. A small part of her wanted to keep
me with her, to saddle me with her own constraints. But I
was also standing in the way of her own path to freedom. Her
impatience to start her new life became entwined with her impatience to get me out of the house.

As I've said, neither she nor my father had the money to
pay for Bradley. The idea was that student loans, combined
with need-based financial aid from Bradley and the govern-
ment financial aid program known as Pell Grants, would cover
the tuition and part of the room and board. If I had to take
out more loans for a private university, then so be it. All of my
friends were taking out loans to go to college. If your family
was rich, you graduated from college without debt, no matter
what your particular gifts were. If your family had below-average
means or was poor, you almost always needed a loan to attend
college—for the most part, no matter what your particular gifts
were.

Exceptions to the iron rule of student loans for the unwealthy
were sometimes made for gifted kids so poor that the college
or university paid their way. These were rare cases, especially in
1975. But though my family had no money, we were not poor.
My mother still had the house. My parents still both had marketable skills and modest incomes. Their social world, such as it
was, still consisted of people at the lower end of the middle class.
And I did not possess, on paper anyway, exceptional gifts.

My mother wrote out my expenses with a pencil on a sheet
of notepaper in her neat, teacher's hand. Along with the income
from the part-time job I would need to get, she said that she
would give me enough money, out of the child support my
father was sending her, to pay the still substantial portion of
room and board that the student loan wouldn't cover. All that
remained was for me to apply for the loan.

One late summer afternoon when I was seventeen, I went
with my mother to the local bank to complete the paperwork

for the borrowed money. My hand shook with excitement as I signed the papers. The impersonal, institutional occasion had an atmosphere of quiet, festive ceremony to it, as my mother looked with gratitude at the banker, and the banker beamed at her and me with an air of being an agent of mobility and positive change. When we finished, the banker, a balding man in his late fifties, shook both our hands.

The celebration continued later that evening when my mother, Nathan, and I met my father at the Suburban Diner, a restaurant on Route 17 that he liked to frequent. My father in particular was jubilant that the bank had approved the loan. Until that moment at the bank the prospect of my going to college was abstract, still open to change. Signing the loan papers made my imminent departure concrete, essentially irreversible.

# 3

# WHAT NOW, VOYAGER?

The Greyhound bus to Chicago left New York City's Port Authority Bus Terminal one evening in late August. By the time it was dark, we were in western Pennsylvania. That was as far west as I had ever been.

If I pressed my head against the window and strained my neck, I could catch sight of dense clusters of stars, more than I had ever seen at one time. Though the night was mild, the air-conditioning on the bus was on full blast. It made the stars seem so distant and cold that I shivered to look at them.

Under the stars the landscape rushing past us was pitch black. I could not understand how such bright things did not shed their light below. I knew next to nothing about how the physical world operated. I detested science's privileging of the facts. In the world of science, the facts of my life would have disqualified me from respect or admiration. I barely passed my high school science courses and retained almost a child's naïveté about the physical world. I conceived of the physical world the way I wanted it to be. I thought the stars were made of pure light.

Directly outside the windows of the bus were dark masses

of trees. Occasionally a watery glow of golden light from a house or houses was visible behind them. The lights made me yearn for home. Not the home I was leaving, but a home situated in the future, still undiscovered. I felt homesick for this undiscovered home that lay further on in time.

Among my cherished sickbed books had been a prose translation of Homer's *Odyssey*. My favorite passage was the one where Odysseus is shipwrecked and washes up onshore. Exhausted, he finds refuge in a grove, between two olive trees, where the goddess Athena "closed his eyelids, and made him lose all memories of his sorrows." Along with wanting to escape from home and broaden my horizons beyond New Jersey, I yearned to find a place to rest and to pull myself together. I sat with my head leaning against the window, watching for the lights as the bus proceeded to Chicago. From there I was to take another bus to Peoria, just under two hundred miles to the south.

Bradley was not far from downtown Peoria, and it was unlike any place I had ever thought I would be. Part of its uniqueness lay in its origins. Bradley had been founded in wealth and sorrow. Lydia Moss Bradley and her husband, Tobias Bradley, made a fortune in banking and real estate in Peoria in the mid-nineteenth century. They were married for thirty years, their union happy and productive. But neither their wealth nor their industriousness protected them from tragedy. By the time Tobias died in 1867, all six of their children had died.

Bereft and alone at the age of fifty, Lydia did not withdraw from the world. She threw herself into humanitarian endeavors that would be supported by the riches she and Tobias had accumulated together.

Lydia and Tobias had explored the possibility of building an orphanage as a tribute to their children. After Tobias's death, Lydia undertook the project by herself. She traveled around the country to visit orphanages. She consulted with people on how best to realize her and Tobias's dreams. Gradually, she expanded her ambitions away from their original plan. She began to envision a place not just of shelter and protection but of empowerment and advancement. According to Bradley's official history, she wanted "to found a school where young people could learn how to do practical things to prepare them for living in the modern world."

The more I read about Bradley, the more I felt drawn toward its aura of Christian stoicism and reserve. The embarrassing and dishonorable truth was that I associated my parents' emotional weakness and lack of emotional restraint with their Jewishness.

Of course what I had in mind was a very specific Russian-Jewishness, Menka's experience of persecution, displacement, and economic hardship. And I was too young to see the multifaceted nature of weaknesses that made me tremble with weakness myself. I could not have seen the way tears and open feeling strengthened these people. Public emoting could scare off some of the world's smaller predators—"Don't you see what you're doing to him? You're playing with fire!"—and it could give the emoter time to think and figure out his next move behind the mask of emoting.

But whatever my nearsightedness about such matters, for me being Jewish meant drama and tears, open vulnerabilities and theatrical admittance of same. Bradley seemed as far from all these as Scandinavia was.

After unspeakable suffering, Lydia Bradley had rolled up her sleeves and immersed herself in nurturing the collective welfare. In 1892, she bought up a majority share of Parsons Horological Institute in La Porte, Indiana. It was the first institution created strictly for the training of watchmakers to be established in America. Not long afterward she moved the institute to her hometown of Peoria. In her will she stipulated that following her death the school be reconfigured to include a classical education, and also education in industrial arts and home economics: "it

being," as she wrote, "the first object of this institution to fur-
nish its students with the means of living an independent, in-
dustrious and useful life by the aid of a practical knowledge of
the useful arts and sciences."

Four years later, William Rainey Harper, the president of
the University of Chicago, persuaded Lydia not to wait until
her own death to honor her children and her husband. In 1897
Bradley Polytechnic Institute opened its doors to the sons and
daughters of the American Midwest who were passionate about
making their way in the world. It became a college in 1920, and
a university in 1946, just in time to welcome masses of maimed
and shell-shocked men returning from war who desired to attend
college on the GI Bill.

Reading the Bradley brochure back home in Paramus,
with my door locked against my mother, who was wailing and
sobbing in her bedroom, I grew excited. Bradley was clearly the
place for me. I overlooked the fact that my father's failure at
Albatross had made me loathe anything having to do with
business, and that I had elevated the intellect and the imagination over the concrete and actual. I felt, with an instinctual at-
traction to the opposite thing, that I could be the beneficiary of
Bradley's emphasis on practical life precisely because I so sorely
needed improvement in that area. Since I despaired of the environment in which I had grown up, Bradley seemed like the ideal
place to go to college.

The hospitable otherness of the school struck me on my very
first day there. After depositing my things in my new dormitory room, I went off to the bursar to cash my student-loan
check. Then I saw the girls. Strong-boned, clear-skinned, with
moist eyes and bouncy, shiny, fragrant hair, they passed by, one
after another. I was entranced. I was entranced with these descendants of pioneers, who blazed through the wilderness in
defiance of every physical and human obstacle. I was in the
midst of an America I'd had no idea existed.

One of the new species of girls, with a light sprinkling of freckles on her cheekbones, was standing on line in front of me. After paying the bursar, she turned and our eyes met. I looked at her and she looked away. Unaware of how ready someone's closely guarded sexuality could be, and of how that made the display of indifference a necessary enticement, I let her walk by me as she left the bursar's window. I paid my bill and then turned to leave. Behind me another girl was waiting. She was slight, fair, with short black hair and small coal-black eyes that were almost all pupil. Her name was Claire Halprin. She was Jewish, from a Chicago suburb. She had come to Bradley to study to be a teacher.

Bradley was, as I said, the only affordable school that I could find that offered an undergraduate degree in journalism. But I did not think of a career in journalism in a conventional way. Having shunned money as a perverse gravitational force that bent people away from their natural destiny, I was determined to make simply living my vocation, the way Erroll Garner made playing the piano a pure expression of who he was. The journalistic practice of transcribing life as it is lived seemed to me the perfect means by which I could make my life my work.

There were no undergraduate degrees in creative writing at the time that I was aware of, and, anyway, I had assimilated, despite all my resistance to it, Menka's and my mother's insistence on finding something that I could "fall back on." So I channeled my love for literature into a halfhearted commitment to journalism. My ability to read well convinced me that I had gifts that were similar to the authors I read. I didn't even think of them as authors, as writers, let alone as artists of any kind. They were human beings who were wise about life. I believed that if I could learn how to perform the journalist's function of illuminating how people lived, then I would find myself in the realm of my cherished Hemingway, Twain, Melville, Joyce, Salinger, Bellow, Ellison, and all the other figures I imagined hovering around me and guiding my destiny.

Still, that did not stop me from writing one maudlin tale after another, each one so laden with big, impressive-sounding words that the language was just one step removed from Latin. One afternoon, seeing my destiny through the ever-hopeful eyes of the Old Man, I even sent one off to a famous magazine. It never responded, but later on, I fabricated some type of actual connection to the magazine by sending it a story every few months and convincing myself, as people do when they buy lottery tickets every week, that sheer persistence would guarantee a breakthrough sooner or later. I stuffed all my stories into my desk drawers after I wrote them. Before I left for Bradley I moved everything to a box that I hid in a corner of the basement.

The bus arrived at the Chicago Greyhound station early the next morning. It was a few hours before I could make the connection to Peoria. I called my mother collect from a pay phone in the station to tell her that I was okay. The movie began playing in her head and she burst into tears. This had the effect of choking me up, too, so I lied and told her that the bus to Peoria was pulling in.

I set down my luggage and took a seat in a row of plastic chairs. A pile of blankets and old ski jackets lay on the floor two chairs away from me. The jackets' white filling was visible in places through the fraying outer shells. I thought that a custodian must have dropped the blankets and clothes there while he made his rounds. Suddenly the pile moved. Two arms and then a head emerged from it. It was a homeless person. His hair was filthy and matted, and his face was so red it looked sunburnt. But I realized that the burn was layers of dirt that had crusted his face and discolored it. He slowly turned his head and looked at me with thick, watery eyes. I jumped up, grabbing my luggage, and hurried, almost running, to a row of chairs on the other side of the station.

I had two suitcases, one large and one small. They were old Samsonite models that had once belonged to my mother. Both of them had faded, peeling decals that said "Bermuda," where my parents had spent their honeymoon. A white-haired woman traveling alone and sitting two seats over from me noticed the decals. Have you been to Bermuda? she asked with what struck me as a new type of tenderness, native to that part of the world. I shook my head. Not yet, I said. Someday. I tried to fall asleep, but could not.

# 4

# HEARTLAND

Tell me what you do with him, I said to Claire Halprin as we lay naked together in her dormitory bed.

We lie in bed, like this, she said.

And what do you do?

He touches me the way you're touching me.

Like this?

Yes.

Does he do this?

Oh. Yes. Yes, he does.

And this?

Ohhhh.

Do you like it when he does that?

Shhhh. Stop talking.

This? You like this?

Yes. Oh, that feels nice.

Does he hold your wrists like this?

Shhhh. Yes, yes.

And he goes into you like this?

Ah! Yes. Ohhh. Yes, yes, he does.

And like this? And this? And this? And this?

Ah, ah, ah. Keep doing it like that.

Kiss me the way you kiss him when he does this to you. Just like that. Is that how he kisses you? Is it? It is, isn't it? Kiss me. Kiss me. Like that. Yes. Yes. Ohhhh. Ohhhh.

Are you finished?

Yeah.

Did it feel nice?

Yes, it did. Was it nice for you?

Yes, it was very nice.

Did you come?

No. But it was nice.

I'm sorry.

For what?

That you didn't come.

It's okay. I liked it.

You didn't like it. I'm sorry. Next time I'll make you come.

Stop. It was fine. Put your hand here. Touch me here. Keep touching me. Yes, like that. Just like that. Softer, softer. Yes, just like that, keep doing it just like that. Ohhh. Ohhhh.

Are you coming?

Yes. Shhhhh. Ohhhh.

Did you come?

Shhhh. Yes.

Do you still see him?

Shhhh. Shhhh.

Claire, do you still see him?

Shhh. Wait a minute.

Do you see him? Tell me.

Wait! I told you. We talk on the phone once in a while, and that's all.

But you never see him.

No, never.

Does he call you or do you call him?

He calls me.

You're a liar.

What?

You're a liar.

How dare you call me that!

I know you called him.

What are you talking about?

Just tell me the truth.

I am telling you the truth. Stop this, please. You're driving me crazy.

I know you're lying because the other day when I came to see you, before I knocked, I heard you—

You were standing outside my door listening to me?

I wasn't listening. I happened to be there.

You happened to be listening!

I happened to be there and heard you call him.

I can't take this anymore.

Just admit it. You called him.

You're insane.

You're making me insane with your lies. Admit it.

Yes, I called him! He called me and I called him back. All right? Nothing is happening between us. You were listening, right? So you know nothing is going on.

I couldn't hear you.

Oh yeah.

And then I knocked and you got off.

I can't take this anymore. He was someone who was in my life so we talk once in a while. It's no big deal. I'm with you. I'm only with you.

It's a big deal for me.

Then go work it out by yourself.

And then the two of you can be together.

Go fuck yourself.

Go ahead. Fuck him all you want. I'm out of here.

I'm not fucking anyone! I'm fucking you!

I'm gone. I can't put up with this shit anymore.

Go ahead.

You want me to go?

I never want to see you again. Get away from me.

You don't mean that.

Oh yes I do.

Where will I go?

That's your problem.

So you do love him. You do!

I don't love anyone. I'm sick of the both of you. I just want everyone to leave me alone.

Aha! You wouldn't be sick of him if you weren't with him. You have to be with someone to be sick of them.

You're sick.

I'm sick in love with you.

No, you're not. You need help.

So help me. I love you, Claire.

Then why do you spy on me and call me a liar?

I don't know.

You have to stop this. You have to start believing me.

I love you. You can do whatever you want. Really. I don't care. I just want to be with you. You can fuck him every night if you want, as long as you come back and fuck me.

I don't want to fuck him!

Yes you do.

You want to fuck him.

Me?

Yes, that's what you want.

I want to fuck *you*.

You want me to fuck *him*.

*You* want to fuck him.

Okay, you're right. I do.

You do!

Yes, I want to fuck him. I'm going to go to him tonight and fuck him and fuck him over and over again.

Do it. Fuck him. I want you to.

No you don't.

Oh yes I do.

Oh no you don't.


Before coming to Bradley, Claire had been at the University of Illinois in Champaign. There she had been involved with an older student, also from Illinois, named Doug. Until I made him the center of our erotic life, he had been safely in her past.


Like me, Claire was the child of divorced parents. Children of divorce often either portray their lives before their parents' breakup as being unhappier than they were, in order to free themselves from guilt over their parents' separation, or idyllic, so that they may think of themselves as being formed by joy rather than misery. Claire fell into the latter category.

Claire's father, she told me, used to arrive home after work, eat dinner, and watch *The Dick Van Dyke Show* with his wife. Then one day he turned the "rec room" into a study, where he sat reading German philosophers like Nietzsche and Schopenhauer—so as to make up for never attending college, he told Claire—until long after his wife went to bed. Next, he was gone.

Claire's mother remarried quickly, in a daze. Her second husband had moved to suburban Illinois from rural Kentucky. Claire's older brother was out of the house by that point. Claire's stepfather swilled beer and raged against her on the slightest pretext. Once he felt secure in the marriage, he began to shout anti-Semitic slurs at her.

Numbed by the rapid replacement of her old life by her

new one, her mother did not have the strength to warn him away. She could not have made it through another separation. She preferred to counsel Claire not to make trouble by defying him. The two of them whispered bitterly and excitedly about him whenever they could. With her daughter she could live out a vicarious rebellion against the new life that she had been dragged into by bad luck, and by her own insolvent will.

I saw Claire's stepfather only once. He had quit his job as a cooling-system technician soon after marrying her mother, who was receiving substantial alimony and child support from her ex-husband. Her second husband had a complex vanity. The image of himself guzzling beer and screaming at a young girl did not suit how he liked to think of himself. So upon learning of Claire's relationship with me, and without having met me, he reconstructed himself as Claire's protector and forbade her to see me. He still screamed at her when he was drinking, but now he declared that it was for her own good, as he railed against what he characterized as my sex-crazed intentions.

I ended up encountering him because during extended weekends, holiday breaks, and summer vacation, I used to park my car, borrowed from new Chicago friends, down the street from Claire's house. She would come meet me at our prearranged time. One evening, when she was nearly an hour late, I drove up to her split-level house. Getting out of the car, I walked along the concrete path across her front lawn toward her front door.

Before I reached her brick and concrete stoop, the door opened. Out walked her stepfather. He was holding a shotgun across his stomach, which bulged under an immaculate white shirt. I kept walking toward the house. Without pointing the gun at me, he stood there, grinning.

Claire's mother appeared in the upstairs window. Please leave! she shouted at me. Just get out of here! Her tone was sharp, so as not to oppose her husband, but the expression on her face was sympathetic, imploring. Claire's face, a small, pale oval, rose up in the window next to her mother's. She blew me a kiss. Raising her wrist to her face, she pointed at her watch. She knew her stepfather had come too far from his old life to jeopardize his new one by killing someone between her real father's automatic sprinklers. Anyway, Orland Park did not seem like the kind of place where someone could ruin himself, go mad, or commit a crime.

Maybe because I was also the child of divorced parents, I was always waiting for the other shoe to drop. I conceived of events as being isolated from each other by inevitable ruptures. This made me unable to grasp the importance of cause and effect in life. What would it have mattered if I had applied myself and done well in high school? Something would have happened to interrupt my smooth progress from there to college, career, and success. Of that I was certain.

Claire was more confident. She knew that she wanted to be a teacher. She arranged her college coursework to achieve her goal. But it was more the goal than the teaching itself that mattered to her. She needed a goal; and teaching presented itself. She frequently talked of following other paths through life: nurse, veterinarian, librarian, social worker. But like me she was poised for disappointment. She felt certain that even a vocation was not likely to last, and that one vocation, so long as it was in line with her temperament, was just as good and fleeting as another.

Working one summer afternoon as a candy striper at a Jewish hospital in Chicago when she was in high school, she was pushing a sick, elderly Orthodox Jew along the corridor in a wheelchair. The man in the wheelchair slowly turned around and stared at her. Are you Jewish? he asked. She smiled and nodded. He looked her over, then he spat on the floor. You're not a Jew, he said.

That was the nature of reality. All of a sudden, where you thought you had a modest stepping-stone into the future you wanted for yourself, you found yourself falling through a trapdoor.

Young veterans of hidden trapdoors and sudden ruptures, Claire and I created our own world where cause and effect did not exist. We created a static realm of pure fantasy. Or rather, I created it. Habituated to solitude in my sickbed, driven further into myself by conflict with my parents, I guided her into the realm of withdrawal.

The two of us inhabited a neatly ordered kingdom, populated by clearly defined good and bad animals. In this made-up universe, nothing happened. Most important, nothing changed. We played word games, fabricated incidents and events, invented other characters—a histrionic wolf, a pathetic panda bear—that had no consequences, possessed no egos, and were invulnerable to changes of heart, personality, or time. We became children again in each other's arms. Doug was meant to be part of our escapist game, another frictionless fantasy.

Along with our similar backgrounds, we shared a growing resistance to Bradley itself. I had not been aware of how dominant a role the fraternities and sororities played in the life of the university. During orientation, over three hot days in late August, when an older student mentioned the robustness of "Greek culture" on campus, I thought he meant that Bradley had a strong classics program.

If you didn't belong to a fraternity or a sorority, you were belittled as a "GDI": a "goddamned individual." Hearing that, I got my back up. The ideal state of being that I strove for and navigated by was my individuality; this, combined with the fact that I was not sure who I was, made up a good part of my personality.

At the same time, like an actor actually becoming who he is pretending to be, my wanting to be sovereign and autonomous imparted those qualities to me, in tiny, mismatched pieces.

Resisting my parents had instilled in me a resistance to any external force that tried to influence my thoughts and feelings. Few types of authority, to my mind, were as menacing as a group of like-minded people.

Still, as with just about every other incoming freshman at Bradley, I was swept down the sluice of "rush week" into one fraternity house after another, as they tried to woo new members, or preened themselves on being wooed. In the weeks before Claire and I became an established couple, I attended the various frat parties in hopes of meeting a girl. Friendless and alone, I was nevertheless elevated by the Old Man's commentary above my discomfort to a plane of gimlet-eyed superiority— "He stood at the party by himself, gazing with a cool eye around the room that was filling up with chimpanzees dressed as humans." However, my sacred individuality did not develop into a romantic asset on these occasions. My gimlet-eyed superiority was lost on the girls I met. I responded by turning to my other incentive for going to the parties, which was to get as drunk as I could.

Even when I was in that condition, the fraternal spirit of those places eluded me. The Greeks and the aspiring Greeks drank with the objective of fusing themselves into one mighty, unified will, capable of impressive feats of confidence building. I, on the other hand, drank to obliterate the social life around me, with the goal of establishing the illusion that the world moved in harmony with what I thought and felt.

I usually left the parties on the early side, not wishing to be stuck there with the fraternity boys. Feeling lonely one night, I lingered. Drunk to the point of numbness, feeling that the room had become a carousel, and just at the edge of stumbling, I made my way upstairs. A crowd of boys were standing outside the narrow doorway of a bedroom. In contrast to the raucous atmosphere, they were hushed and mostly still. Some of them politely pushed their way forward now and then to try to peer into the bedroom.

Unwilling to attract attention to myself, I resisted the impulse to find out what was happening and stayed just beyond the small crowd. One of the boys standing outside the door leaned forward and supported himself by gently placing his arm on the back of the boy standing in front of him. The impersonal intimacy of his gesture, the group tenderness of it, nurtured by whatever forbidden thing was happening in the bedroom, infuriated me.

I stormed down the narrow staircase, seething against the fraternities. Hatred was an old reflex that won me a measure of superiority to my environment. Yet even as the alcohol was filling my head with fantasies of violence and rescue, I could not get the bedroom out of my mind. You consciously abide by your finest instincts and then up rises this vague, weightless countercurrent of depravity running inside you: base, beyond thought, a sensation rather than a feeling, disgusting.

I spent the next night with Claire in her dorm room. I did not tell her about the unseen, unknown incident that had taken root in my mind, only about the indignation that the frat boys aroused in me. She listened with kindness and understanding. That was when I started to fall in love with her.

The school that Lydia Bradley had envisioned as a place to prepare for living a practical life in the modern world was, if anything, more successful at achieving its objective than she might have wished it to be. The combination of fraternity culture and the school's obvious preferences for business majors mastering the skills of grabbing and getting, and for basketball stars, reduced the atmosphere on campus to a biological dimension. It was as if, after the deaths of her children, behind Lydia's decent aspirations for the place lay her unconscious urge to ensure that the strongest and the fittest survive at all costs.

As for the journalism department, it turned out to offer a handful of courses taught by one or two indifferent instructors. It was nothing like the intensive major the brochure had advertised.

The bright side of all this was that Bradley's small preserve of the humanities became the beneficiary of a business culture's vain largesse. Bradley had constructed a special reading room in the library that housed the timeless works of literature and philosophy on mahogany bookshelves. Brass lamps glowed softly on long polished-wood tables. The carpet was deep red, crimson.

I tried to read my way through Western civilization there night after night, staying later and later as I became increasingly alienated from my roommate, Tad, a business major from a small Illinois town. He belonged to a fraternity, and I enjoyed mocking Greek culture to him. One weekend afternoon, I was playing an Erroll Garner record that my father had left behind in his hasty departure from the split-level house in Paramus, and that I had spirited off with me to Illinois. Without a word, Tad rose from his bed, where he'd been reading the newspaper, lifted the record, and tossed it onto my bed at my feet. This was the climax of the smoldering tension between his unbearably affable manner and my unbearably arrogant one. I leapt up and pushed him against the wall. He marched down to the resident advisor, who sent me to the dean of students. There I was told by a hastily assembled committee that if I attacked Tad again, I would be sent to the school psychologist.

This was too bad because I thought that Tad, who served as an emergency medical services volunteer back in his hometown, was the sort of guy who would sacrifice his life to save someone so long as you didn't challenge his rigid sense of right and wrong. His inflexible morality was what made him potentially a hero. It

was the herdlike quality of his morality that made me unable
to accept it. Tad was one of the most decent guys I'd ever met.
Still, I couldn't stand him.

On the other hand, I would have fought to the death on
behalf of the books I read in that special collections room with
its bloodred carpet, books so many of which were essentially
deflations of any claim to heroism that did not acknowledge
humankind's essential baseness, viciousness, and inadequacy.

Unable to fit into the campus mainstream, I moved toward
people who also stood out at various angles from Bradley's general population. One of them was Thomas. We lived on the same
dormitory floor. Soon after we became friends, I began to escape
Tad by spending time with Thomas in his room.

When I came to visit at night, he turned off the lights and
lit candles, which produced a scent like exotic food. Thomas's
pale skin bordered on the luminescent. In the candlelight, his
radiant white skin beneath his black hair seemed like a poetic
frame for the upside-down candle situation he was in at Bradley, his true predilections now flickering into view, now flickering away.

I first thought, in the manner of adolescents back then, that
he was one of those odd boys who acted like a girl—nothing
more than that. It wasn't until much later that I realized he
was struggling to be inconspicuously gay at a school where the
faintest trace of effeminacy got you shouldered into the side of
a building if you had the bad luck to be walking alone toward
the wrong people late on a liquor-soaked weekend night.

He also had the half-misfortune of hailing from a small town
somewhere in the southern part of Illinois. It was only half-bad
because, as he explained to me, one part of a small town has its
special mechanisms for protecting outsiders who have been stig-

matized by another part. He laughed with a rare flash of bitterness when he said that. He aspired as much as I did to be saved by cosmopolitanism and intellectual enlightenment.

I myself never associated his femininity with his sexuality. To me, as a seventeen-year-old boy, he was a "fairy." But I did not think of him as being a "faggot." With the exception of advanced personalities like Alex Tarmanian and Teddy Di Buono, both of them perhaps evolved by sophisticated music into a deeper humanity, where I came from "fairy" meant not like other boys, but "faggot" meant malevolent fairy.

In neither case, though, did the image of two boys or men making love come to mind. My friends and I knew the term "homosexual," but that was a whole other plane of meaning. Whereas "fairy" elicited our giggles and "faggot" our sneers, "homosexual" caused a mystified hush to descend upon us. As long as being gay was a question of style or manner diametrically different from ours, we could laugh or mock it away. Its true meaning, half-perceived and resisted by us, as another way to love and to have sex, flustered us into silence. After a while I stopped thinking of Thomas as a fairy and started thinking of him, somewhat nervously, as "strange and sensitive."

On those nights when I spent time with him in his room, Thomas lit the candles and talked to me about books he was in thrall to at the moment. A book he was especially fond of was a collection of short stories. He loved one story in particular. He read it to me several times, always pausing to relish this line: "With her little lacquer brush, while the phone was ringing, she went over the nail of her little finger, accentuating the line of the moon." He liked to repeat the final cadence: "accentuating the line of the moon."

Moon, June, croon, loon, he said.

Cautious about who he really was, he had to eke himself out to me slowly. As if his metabolism found the way to do this on its own, his face shone more intensely when he talked to me. It was like a lightbulb that burns brighter after being banged, just before it goes out.

What do you make of the moon, Lee? he asked me one night when there was a full moon in the nighttime sky outside the window. He leaned forward with a smile, trying to be sophisticated and provocative. Instead he appeared vulnerable and transparent. The vulnerability of someone who thought he was mastering a situation, but wasn't, cut right through me.

I like the moon, I said, shrugging uncertainly.

What do you think is on the dark side of the moon? he asked me. He stressed the word "dark," as if it was both exciting and ironic.

I had heard the phrase "dark side of the moon," but being scientifically apathetic, I had never actually connected it to a physical reality that was part of the moon itself until that moment.

All sorts of wild and wonderful things? I said. His strangeness intimidated me. I hoped to please him. What do *you* think is on the other side? I asked.

He looked at me with that mixture of forced excitement and irony. The same as what's on the light side, he said. Then, bending toward me in self-spiting, vindictive impersonation of the frightening weirdo people treated him as back home, and with a theatrical whisper, he said: Just harder to see.


The friendship with Thomas didn't extend beyond my nighttime visits to his room; some friendships require special lighting. There were two other boys with whom I had fuller relationships. One was Simon Cahill, who had grown up in Oak Park, Illinois. I don't remember where I first met him. I think it was in my Milton class, but maybe that would be too richly ironic to be true. Milton was famously Protestant, while everyone on both sides of

Simon's family was Irish-Catholic as far back as you could go. Simon had gone to Catholic schools all his life, and he reignited my fascination with the atmosphere of Catholic ritual that Matthew Cassidy and his family had sparked in me a decade earlier.

Simon's head was lopsided. It was as if fate had gnawed on it for a while before casting it aside. His eyes were barely more than slits; to this day, I'm not sure whether they were brown or blue. At drunken parties, especially frat parties, boys would sometimes taunt him or give him a push. Emboldened by the alcohol, I would come up beside Simon and scream Fuck off! at them. Sometimes his tormentors backed away. More often than not, Simon had to step between them and me and wave them off as though they were a flock of crows. His blustering, cumbersome largeness created a startling effect. The other boys converted their aggression into scornful laughter and we were spared. No one really wanted a fight.

Simon's face had a mournful appearance. This sorrowful effect was accentuated by a head of rich, wavy dark-red hair that fell over his shoulders. His hair, his physical softness—he seemed to have been piled into a large sack—and his full, drooping lips gave him a feminine aspect. In fact anytime he witnessed a Thomas-like person being spat at or pushed on campus, his face took on a stricken expression. He shook his long head with surprising anger. But he seemed to have no appetite for any type of person in particular; only a vast, general yearning. I had the sense that he pitied Claire for being with me, and me for believing that she was in love with me. He and she became good friends.

On several occasions Simon brought me home with him to his family's tidy bungalow-style house in Oak Park on long weekends and, in one case, for a week during the summer. His height must have derived from an earlier ancestor because his parents were both smaller than he. They seemed in fantastic shape for people in their late forties: slender, ruddy-faced, their eyes sparkling with vitality.

After a while, though, you brushed up against them or put your arms around them to say hello or goodbye and you realized that their slenderness was made up of stringy muscles and sinews. Their faces were flushed, and their eyes seemed trapped in a shiny viscous liquid. They were both alcoholics, and they were dying. Some people become clearer and clearer as they die, almost transparent. Simon's parents had a desiccated translucency.

They were drunk when they came down to their small kitchen for lunch, drunk as you passed by them in the afternoon. At dinner, as they elaborated on the wonders of Chicago for me, and the magical visit they once made to New York, and the joy of being alive, they each had several glasses of wine. After dinner, still celebrating all the colorful places and personalities they had found in life, they each had three martinis. They never went to sleep; they passed out.

Simon himself hated alcohol, feared it, and refused to discuss it beyond that. He drank, and drank a lot, because it was in his genes and he could not resist it. This fatal succumbing to an inherited yet foreign part of his nature was probably what accounted for the expression of sorrow on his face.

During my stays in Oak Park, Simon introduced me to his closest friend, bespectacled, quiet, scholarly Duncan. They had been friends all through the many years of Catholic school. The two of them entertained me with stories of apoplectic nuns and Jesuit priests in sharkskin suits who drove around in Cadillacs with their girlfriends. One time, they told me, the two of them decided to take a rowboat across Lake Michigan to Canada. It began to storm, and they would have drowned if they had been farther away than the twenty feet from shore it had taken them all morning to get to.

With Simon, who aspired to be a photographer, I spent a

good deal of time in Chicago's museums. At night we sat in his kitchen, drinking ourselves numb and talking about Hemingway, who grew up in Oak Park, and Frank Lloyd Wright, who designed several houses there. Simon remarked on the similarity between Hemingway's spare, flat prose and the straightforward verticality presented by the town's row upon row of oak trees. He connected both to Frank Lloyd Wright's sincere planes—half-Japanese, half-midwestern prairie. Simon's parents were overgrown children who drank out of helplessness, the alcohol devouring their self-destructive innocence and corrupting their transparency. In unconscious response, Simon was profoundly moved by sober sincerity and clarity. When we were ready for bed, we put our arms around each other for support and quietly climbed the stairs to our bedrooms on the second floor.

The other boy I became close to was Eduardo Caravantes. His family was Mexican. They had emigrated to Chicago when he was a small child. Eduardo grew up on Chicago's south side, in a neighborhood known as "back of the yards" because it was located directly behind where the city's famous slaughterhouses once stood before they were relocated to Joliet, fifty miles to the south.

Chicago cops, Eduardo told me, used to drag him and his brother, Mauricio, onto the slaughterhouse grounds and beat them for fun. They got beaten like "little hamburgers," Eduardo said, his eyes wide not with pain at the memory, or a sense of drama or fascination with his own story, or detached amusement. I could never figure out why his eyes widened like that.

At a certain point, Eduardo's reactions drifted away from what he was saying and from the situation he was reacting to. He was eccentric, perhaps a little unhinged. He laughed often, yet he had no sense of humor. The warmth of his laughter made up for it. He liked to wear an old green army jacket and refer to

himself as Hawkeye, after the character in the TV series
*M\*A\*S\*H*, about a medical unit in Korea during the Korean
War. Eduardo wanted passionately to be a doctor, though you
couldn't be sure whether it was a fantasy inspired by the TV
show, or a genuine aspiration on account of which he was drawn
to the show. What was clear was that between his odd discon-
nectedness and his struggles to keep up with his science classes,
he faced a difficult path to medical school.

Eduardo's pathos was what drew me to him. Failure, or the
near certainty of it, seemed to me concrete evidence of someone's
humanity. Wealth and privilege, on the other hand, were the
conditions for heartlessness. Magnanimity generated by material good fortune was, to my mind, merely shrewd cover for the
driving ambition that accrued and sustained the material
wealth. I thought I detected this calculating social intelligence
whenever I encountered scions of old midwestern families at
Bradley. Another person's ambition had no room for me with
all my emotional needs and embarrassing shortcomings. Rich
people were too used to advancing on forward-sliding circumstances and with forward-moving people to pause with someone who had no advancing motion to offer them at all.

The best people, the ones you could count on, were the ones
who needed other people. Their need for others guaranteed that
they would treat you decently. To need other people meant that
you had a weak spot inside you that required shoring up. The bigger the weakness, the greater the need; the greater the need, the
larger the decency and compassion. There was room for me in
Thomas's half-concealed injuries and shame, in Simon's sorrowful face, in Eduardo's impoverished background.

Perhaps these special criteria of mine were just a way to
shape my emotions into the same sort of expediencies I deplored
in people who were materially well situated. But whatever the
selfishness that might have been at its source, my radar for wound
detection opened me up to others. My heart went out to Ed-

uardo. Having been showered with financial aid by Bradley, he
felt academically vulnerable. As I had with Tina Durrell, I
thought I could lend him my support, or at least make him feel
good about himself. He struggled with his literature papers and
I stayed up night after night helping him write them. In return,
Eduardo, who could see my distress, consoled me on the nights
when I couldn't sleep. Once in a while, he lent me money, too,
when my mother's checks failed to arrive.

Though about once a month my mother sent me a check for a
hundred dollars, I could not meet all my monthly expenses without working. As I had planned on doing even before leaving for
Bradley, I applied for and landed a job at Bergner's department
store in Peoria within weeks of my arriving at school. I worked
there three nights a week and all day on Saturday until an incident that occurred one evening in the middle of winter.

I had been hired to work as a salesman in the men's department. The salesman I was replacing taught me how to fit jackets
and pants, and how to make alterations marks with a piece of
chalk. That evening a customer I had waited on returned to the
store to pick up and try on a pair of pants he had bought. Exiting
the fitting room wearing the pants, he complained to me that
they were so tight that he couldn't fasten the clasp.

Come over here, I said. Let's see what's wrong.

He was a big man; large-framed, not overweight. He must
not have bought a nice pair of pants for a long time because he
seemed astonished and on the verge of outrage that the pants
didn't fit. As usual, no matter who the person was whose expectations I had to satisfy, and no matter his moral position, I began to worry about displeasing him. As they always did when I
was nervous, my telltale hands began to shake.

In some pairs of pants there is a spare bit of material around
the waistband that can be tightened or loosened. I put my hands

into the back of his pants and let some out. This had the effect of loosening the pants too much around the waist, so I pulled the material tighter. Unfortunately, I did not realize, because the customer did not tell me, that the tightness was not around his waist but in his crotch. When I made the pants tighter, he cried out in distress. I had been kneeling, as I had seen other tailors do back in Bamberger's in Paramus. Instinctively, in pain, he pushed me and I fell back onto the floor. You hurt me, you ass-hole, he cried.

The department manager rushed over to pacify him, offer-ing to give him his pants for free, with the corrective alterations on the house. I got off with a stern warning. But the scolding stung me, not only because the manager was only a few years older than I was but because I needed the job. I was also angry at myself for not having mastered the technique of making the alterations marks.

Still, I felt resentful that the manager had not stuck up for me after I made what I considered to be an innocent mistake. I sensed resentment on his part, too. I could see that he had moved me mentally into the "potential pest" category. He had no feel-ings for or against me. He only wanted to have as much peace and quiet in his life as possible. He simply didn't realize that pursuing peace and quiet was a full-time, nerve-rattling job.

The tax on his time and nerves happened a few months later, near closing time. A man gathered up an armload of shirts and made a run for the front door.

I heard the manager shouting as he ran out from the altera-tions room onto the floor of the men's department.

Catch him! he screamed at me. Get him!

I stood there, moving my head this way and that to keep the shoplifter in sight.

You! he said to me. Go after him!

Me? I said.

Go after him! he cried.

The shoplifter was about to reach the door.

He's almost out of the store, I said.

Well, go get him! the manager shouted. He walked to the edge of the men's department platform. Eat me! he screamed at the shoplifter.

I watched as the thief flung open the glass door and barreled out onto the street.

Get him!! the manager was shrieking at me. He had forgotten about the shoplifter, except as the occasion to shriek at me.

It's too late, I said. He's out of the store.

The manager's face was crimson.

Then you get out there after him! Now! He's in the parking lot! That's store property!

I doubt it, I said. He's probably out of the parking lot. Or he's driving away in a car.

Go after him. The manager's voice had returned to its normal range. I don't know whether your unchanging character leads you to go through life having similar experiences, or you classify experiences according to similar ones you've had, but his soft tone reminded me of the sheriff who had paid the visit to our house the year before. He didn't have to shout. If I didn't run out of the store to apprehend someone for taking a few pieces of merchandise, I would be fired. Now that he was in a position to exercise an ultimate authority over me, he was perfectly calm.

No, I said. I'm not going to do that.

He winced slightly, but then he smiled.

Don't forget to cash out before you leave, he said over his shoulder as he walked away. The following Friday I had a note in my paycheck telling me that I had been let go.


Claire quickly got me a job as a short-order cook at a diner where she was working as a waitress. Her father had stopped sending child support when Claire turned eighteen. I met him just once.

Over dinner in a restaurant to which he took Claire and me in Gary, Indiana—where bluish-yellow flames fluttered out of slender smokestacks like pilot lights under a metallic stovetop sky—he hectored me with an analysis of his favorite quote from Schopenhauer, once I told him that I was interested in philosophy: "Money is human happiness in the abstract. He who is no longer capable of enjoying human happiness in the concrete devotes himself utterly to money."

I am utterly incapable of enjoying human happiness, said Mr. Halprin. I am very rich, he said, with megalomaniacal self-disparagement, and I am very empty. He turned to Claire. My daughter suffers as a result, he said. He kissed her on the top of her head.

Have you ever had frog legs? he asked me. He placed a proprietary arm around her. They were sitting on a banquette. I was on a chair beside Claire.

No, I said.

They're delicious, he said. I'll order some for you.

No thanks, I said.

You're afraid to, he said. He gave Claire, who was still sitting inside his embrace, a conspiratorial little jiggle with his arm.

No, I replied. And, I said excitedly, ambitiously, Spinoza would agree with Schopenhauer. He said that money was the abstract of everything.

That's bullshit, he said. Money is money. Nothing is the abstract of anything. I'll order the frog legs for you.

Then he said: You're clearly an expert on Spinoza. But what's your philosophy?

I didn't even have to think about that one.

Do it to him before he does it to you, I said. That was Marlon Brando in *On the Waterfront*. He was telling Eva Marie Saint his, as he called it, "philosophy of life." I had convinced myself that it was mine, too.

Have you ever done that? he said.

Done what? I asked him.

Done it to someone before they did it to you, he said.

I stared at him helplessly. Claire squeezed my hand.

That's also bullshit, he said.

On the bus back to Peoria, Claire buried her face in my chest, and I sank my face into her soft black hair. For the first time, she told me that she loved me. As for me, "I love you" had become my war cry. I had been declaring it to her almost since we first met.

I worked at the diner until I left Bradley. I eventually got fired from the diner, too, though aside from the time I spit into a chicken sandwich that a customer had returned after insulting Claire, I can't think of any friction, or unpleasantness.

I do remember Dino, who owned the place, teaching me how to determine the tenderness of a steak. This was his method: You make a tight fist and push the skin between your thumb and forefinger. That's well done. Relax your fist a little and push again. That's medium. Relax it a lot. Push. That's rare. After working at the diner, I liked to joke that I saw myself and everyone I met as a dish fit for the gods, except that we all seemed pretty indigestible. Yuk, yuk, yuk.

By the time my first college summer came around, I had decided not to return home. I missed my friends, especially Paul, but the thought of living with my mother again sank my spirits.

My chief reason, though, for staying in the Midwest was that I needed to be near Claire. I had invested in her the family feelings that had been orphaned by the troubled relationships with my mother and my father. She saw me as a nice, funny, intelligent, strange, and troubled boy who might or might not be someone she could have a future with. For me, she was companion, lover, savior, mother, friend, nurse. With me, she went out on dates. With her, I was on a life-or-death journey.

Claire went home every summer to live with her mother and stepfather in Orland Park. Since staying with her was obviously not a possibility, I needed someone who would put me up in or around Chicago. That was how, at the end of May, in 1976, I went to live for three months with Eduardo and his family on Chicago's South Side. When I had timidly dropped the hint to Eduardo that I needed a place to stay in Chicago, I said that I only expected to stay part of the summer. Eduardo insisted, with his usual generosity and that disconnected laugh of his, that I spend the entire summer with him.

Poverty is a condition that consumes your insides. Lacking money is a circumstance. You adapt to poverty, so that even as you are struggling to escape it, you are strengthening the forces keeping you there. Tomorrow, and tomorrow, and tomorrow are all the same. The sameness is why poor people are often wearing heavy winter coats on the first warm days of spring. They exist in a permanent season of vulnerability. If, on the other hand, you lack money but are not poor, tomorrow is another day with its own specific coordinates. You wear shorts on a warmish day in early March because you are adapting to the weather outside you, and not surrendering to the damp cold in your soul.

Lacking money is a material situation, but the disease of poverty is that it is ultimately intangible. It enters your metabolism and lurks everywhere: in your absence of confidence, in your fear of getting sick, in your pessimism, in your impulsiveness, in how you gratify yourself, and how you protect yourself. In the same way, the power of terrorism lies in its capacity to infiltrate a mood or emotion. Poverty is a type of terror.

My parents began by lacking money and slowly descended toward the condition of being poor. My father, especially, seemed

more and more comfortable adapting to a condition of depriva-
tion than seeing financial setback as another temporary event
in life.

Eduardo's family was poor. The amount of money they possessed had little to do with their circumstances. They had mysterious infusions of money one day, and were just getting by
the next, but even when they were flush, they acted rashly, wor-
ried excessively, were helplessly drawn for all their dreams of a
better life to the worst scenario, and felt most comfortable with
people in similar material circumstances. As for me, I took to the
hard-pressed anarchic life of the Caravantes family like a fish to
a different tank of water.

Eduardo's parents were divorced. His father worked as a
foreman in a cheese factory, which he had also made his home,
sleeping on a cot in his office. Eduardo lived in a dilapidated
row house with his mother, his three brothers, and his sister. I
never learned his two younger brothers' given names because
the other members of the family only referred to them by their
nicknames: Gordo, meaning "the fat one," for the older of the
two; and Flaco, meaning "the skinny one," for the younger boy.

The youngest child was Susanna. She was twelve, and she
spent the day sweeping, vacuuming, dusting, taking out the garbage, and working in the kitchen. Susanna was adopted. After
so many sons, Eduardo's mother, Perla, needed someone to help
her with the work of raising them, and also to assist her in main-
taining the house, which was under constant siege by her ram-
paging youngest boys. During the day, I could hear Perla barking
commands at Susanna, or snapping at her when the girl failed
to follow instructions or to fulfill a certain task. At night, however, Susanna experienced a transformation. She became the true
daughter that Perla longed for in a corner of her bustling, hus-
tling heart, where love had turned her into a ruthless adminis-
trator. At night, her broom and dustpan tucked away in the hall
closet downstairs, Susanna spent hours in her mother's room as

Perla braided her long black hair, and the two of them traded gossip and told stories to each other.

Apart from everyone else, yet vital to their fragile cohesion as a unit, was Mauricio, the oldest son. Mauricio was the family's quiet center of gravity. He was another person for whom silence and soft speaking were hallmarks of his power.

In the absence of a father, Mauricio was both precocious partriarch and the family's hope and pride: its future. Tall and well built, he had a different physical aspect from his siblings. An Indian influence was much stronger in him. Eduardo had amiable good looks that immaturity had softened into a boy-ishness that made people overlook or ignore him. Mauricio, as if in some contrast premeditated by a higher power, possessed high, strong cheekbones, an angular face, and steady gray eyes. He rarely smiled, and even more rarely laughed, but when he smiled or laughed, it was always because something genuinely pleasant or humorous had occurred.

Of all the siblings, Mauricio most resembled Perla. It was as if she had passed on the essence of herself to him, leaving traces of it for his brothers. Perla was a large woman with fair skin and thick black hair. She was about six feet tall and had shoul-ders like a fullback. The exertion of childbearing seemed to have taken the greater physical toll on her ex-husband, father of all her children. He was reedlike and small, as if drained and shrunk by the effort of producing four sons. But divorce, raising five children, struggling to earn a living had worn Perla out. Her eyes, by the late afternoon, were half-closed and wet with fatigue.

When I knew her, she had an Italian boyfriend named Gino. Perla was in her midforties and he was in his early sixties. One afternoon I walked into the living room, thinking I was the only one in the house. Gino jumped up from the sofa, struggling to pull his pants up from where they had fallen over his shoes, and fell onto his face. Perla rose from the sofa, tugging on her

skirt, her face flushed. Both of them laughed richly. Inviting
me to drink brandy with them, they drew me into a conversation about Claire. The slightest lull in her feelings about me
drove me into despair. Lately I had been spending part of the
evening in the Caravanteses' living room, drinking beer and
staring into space. *Las mujeres!* Perla would say to me, laughing.
*No pueden vivir con ellas, no pueden vivir sin ellas!* Then she would
slap Gino on the leg and leave the two of us sitting there by
ourselves, smiling to each other shyly, without anything to say.


Perla survived by the grace of Chicago's mayor Richard J. Daley,
who was in the last year of his twenty-three-year reign over
Chicago. He died of a heart attack that winter. Daley had put
Perla on his payroll. In return she worked as one of his opera-
tives in the Mexican American community on the South Side,
rounding up votes for Daley and the other officials who were
part of the machine he ran that ruled Chicago. The great thing
about working for Daley, Eduardo told me, was that you didn't
have to work at all. Perla seldom went to an office. Instead, during that summer anyway, she conferred with her sons on an
individual basis throughout the day, drank and made love with
Gino, disappeared and suddenly reappeared, sometimes sweeping
into the house with a new coffeemaker, or a vacuum for Susanna,
or accompanied by a delivery man toting a new television up the
stairs behind her. Then she would vanish again, leaving Susanna
in the kitchen amid the smells of onions, cilantro, and chocolate
simmering in a sauce on the stove.

Perla lived from one isolated moment to the next, her com-
ings and goings enigmatic, without order or structure or fore-
seeability, swept along from one contingency to the next, one
need to the next. Decades later I would, briefly, from time to
time, encounter celebrities, rich and famous people, who lived
in the same way. I suppose that absolute excess of money and

absolute deficiency of money sometimes create the same freedom from predictable patterns of existence—the crucial difference being the certainty, or not, of capital behind and below
you, which also is the difference between a sense of freedom
making you feel that you are flying, and a feeling of being unmoored that gives you the illusion of being free. One evening
in July, leaping from the valley of one moment to the precipice
of another, Eduardo's father took the two of us out to dinner
at the Pump Room, one of Chicago's most expensive and most
fashionable restaurants. Then he returned to his cot in the cheese
factory.

Gordo and Flaco were too young too work. Eduardo found a
summer position as a full-time assistant in a biology lab that
processed medical tests. Mauricio also aspired to be a doctor,
but he had a year-round job in the Chicago police gym. His acceptance by the Chicago police force, composed then mostly of
Irish American cops, served as a kind of vindication for him.
After performing his duties there, which consisted of keeping
everything in order and occasionally spotting for some of the
cops when they pressed weights on the bench, Mauricio worked
out himself, keeping to a strict schedule. He turned the robust
physique he had inherited from his mother into something
nearly statuesque. His striking looks and his air of understated
authority won him a captivating Mexican girfriend named Laura.
She responded to my ogling stares by directing at me an occasional commiserating pout. Your *guero* looks so serious, she would
tell Mauricio in front of me.

Ever since coming to the Midwest, I had spoken to my
mother on the phone once every few weeks. Before I left Peoria for Chicago, she informed me that since she assumed that
I was going to be working full-time in Chicago all summer, as

I had mentioned to her, she was going to discontinue her inter-
mittent checks to me until school started up again in the fall.
When I protested, she began to sob and accused me of sucking
her dry.

It would be years before I got either a checking or a savings
account, and not until my forties did I, fleetingly, possess a
credit card. I arrived at the Caravanteses' without a penny to
my name. Perla, seeing my situation, began stuffing twenty-
dollar bills into my pockets, to Eduardo's embarrassed delight,
and Mauricio's obvious distaste. She had spent so many years
living her life in circumvention of the fluctuating presence of
money that when money came, she did not establish a practical
relationship to it. She put it at the disposal of whatever her
immediate need was, no matter how wasteful, trivial, or unre-
lated to her self-interest. Her relationship to money moved me.

I was grateful for her generosity to me and then, in tiny
increments of self-absorption, I started to expect money from
her. I even asked her once for enough money to take Claire to
dinner and the movies, which she gave to me with a sly smile.
The next day, she happily announced to me that she had found
me a position at a medical book warehouse on the other side
of town.

That became my summer job. I awoke at dawn, took a bus
to another bus, and waited outside the warehouse with the other
employees for Ned, the manager, to arrive and let everyone in.

My responsibilities were to unload crates of books when they
came in, and then to put the books in the right place on the
vast rows of metal shelves. Though the work was boring, I
threw myself into it. Running and working out in the gym had
not yet become ways of life, and it had been years since I played
sports. Hauling books back and forth on large dollies and in

handcarts, loading boxes into the narrow metal platform that served as an elevator, shelving thousands of books a day, I felt renewed by physical effort.

But I could not keep myself from taking furtive breaks now and then to read the medical books. I pored over heavy textbooks detailing heart ailments, every type of cancer, gastric maladies, bone fractures, gunshot wounds, bedsores, degenerative muscular conditions, and on and on through every variation of illness in the parallel yet separate life of the body. I was especially fascinated by the accompanying photographs: bedsores in the shape of flowers, dementia-causing tangles in the brain, plaque accumulating into what looked like snowdrifts inside the arteries. I could not take my eyes off the photographs of psoriasis in all its forms. My skin still erupted from time to time and seeing my condition delineated by the camera had a therapeutic effect similar to recognizing my troubles in a novel. The extreme cases of the disease, in which the skin hardens into calluses that resemble slabs of concrete, filled me with horrified relief. You are never fully aware of your body until some component of it breaks down, and then the terms of existence are suddenly reversed: your intellect and your consciousness become useless appendages, and your body starts thinking and speaking in pain and in resistance to pain. Reading and gazing at the medical textbooks while in possession of my health strengthened the illusion, so precious to me, of the sovereignty of my intellect and consciousness as they stood apart from the appalling data in my hands.

Sometimes Ned, who periodically patrolled the warehouse's several floors, caught me as I was absorbed in the books. Ned had graduated from the University of Chicago two decades earlier with a degree in English literature. Rather than admonishing me for reading on the job, he was happy to find me in an indolent moment, because it meant drawing me into a short conversation about literature. He adopted a kidding, faux mentorly tone with me. The basis of optimism, he would quote as he play-fully wagged a scolding finger, is sheer terror. I loved that one. Then, with a mildness rooted in complicity with me, he would instruct me to return to work.

Ned intrigued me. Witty, intelligent, and deeply cultured, he was unable to find a paying niche in life that corresponded to his rich personal qualities. Somehow he drifted into manag-ing the medical book warehouse. He didn't like the job, yet he eased into his daily duties with what looked for all the world like contentment. His dry skin was the color of Dentyne. He chain-smoked Pall Mall cigarettes, which had no filters. He settled comfortably into his uncomfortable position at the warehouse as the wry, cultivated, gently caustic supervisor of people who were not cultivated, wry, or caustic. If you said something that pleased him, he looked down at the ground and smiled to himself, as if giving you a lesson in his nature, which was rueful and ironic. His standing at an ironic angle to everyone else, his mildly caus-tic self-distancing, the striking air of solitariness about him that was nevertheless a type of invitation, made me assume that, like Thomas, he had a different life from the standard version.

Ned rented an apartment in Hyde Park, the University of Chicago neighborhood where he had lived when he was a stu-dent. His favorite story was about Bruno Bettelheim, the famous Austrian American child psychologist. Bettelheim's apart-ment was across an alley from Ned's. Every day at three, the neighborhood children arrived home from school and began playing in the alley. And every day at three, Bettelheim, the distinguished child psychologist, threw open his window and screamed down at the children in a heavy Austrian accent: "Shaaaht aaahpp!!"

Ned had a fondness for undercutting whatever was conven-tionally admired. His very existence was proof that the personal qualities society claimed to value—wit, kindness, intelligence—society had no interest in sustaining if those qualities were all a person had to offer. The grossly disillusioning medical text-books were a great setting for him. Perhaps my own deadly earnestness about books and ideas marked me as another person headed for the margins and that was why, shyly, discreetly, Ned did whatever he could to protect me at the warehouse.

I needed, if not protection, some kind of vigilance about me since I was one of only two white warehousemen on the floor. This was at a time when Chicago was still Balkanized. Eduardo had laid down for me the local dangers, which I understood in the following way: Mexicans or blacks would be murdered if they went to the white-ethnic enclave of Marquette Park; Mexicans would meet their demise in Marquette Park or along black Ashland Avenue; whites would be killed along Ashland Avenue or—without protectors—in the Mexican back of the yards; and black people, basically, would end up dead wherever they were.

In the warehouse, the rest of the workers were divided into Mexicans and blacks. The two groups never interacted, even when they had to work side by side. On breaks they kept to themselves in parts of the warehouse that each group had staked out for itself. It was a little like a prison yard. Some of the Mexicans and blacks had the fantasy muscles of people who had been in the unreal nightmare of jail, where I imagined prisoners turning themselves into machines of superhuman density for the purpose of warding off other prisoners, and also to drive out excruciating prison time by using clockwork motions to make their bodies solid, and to rival the solid walls that confined them. The idea of prison terrified me.

Both groups regarded me with hostile indifference or benign amusement. For my part, I was drawn to each of them for different reasons. The kindness with which Eduardo and his family treated me made me think that I shared an affinity with all Mexicans, especially in Chicago. And the association that I made in my mind of my grandfather with the black porters of Grand Central Station, along with the sympathetic bonds I had formed in Alexander's, convinced me that the black workers would warm to me sooner or later. I was thrown for a loop when, sitting not far from the black group during our lunch break, I heard them boasting about shooting "gooks." They had all been together in Vietnam, I learned then. The experience of authorized killing, after years of being the targets of authorized violence, had empowered them. They glowed like gods when they talked about it.

I spoke to my father by phone once in a great while. He had lost his new real estate job and had returned to teaching piano. Depression made him speak so softly that I could barely make out what he was saying. His habit of remaining silent where once he might have stuttered also complicated our conversations. He still called me Lee-boy and spoke romantically about my experience at Bradley. I bet you're knocking them dead, he said to me; I bet you have to fight off all the girls. Prolonged setback and naive romantic expectations had divided him into two people. He said bright and optimistic things in tones muffled by despair.

I was more frequently in touch with my mother. Increasingly, my relationship with her revolved around money: money, in my eyes, that she had promised to send me and that I felt she owed me; money, in her eyes, that she really didn't have, or that she believed she was entitled to hold on to. Slowly she moved me into the same column as Menka and my father. Both of them, in their different ways, had deadened her desires. She had tried to bring her desires to life again by fighting over money. She fought about money with Menka, who accused her of bringing herself to the brink of penury by divorcing my father. She fought about money with my father, who was now unable to meet his child-support obligations, his only source of income the piano lessons he was giving each week. Before long, my mother seemed to live for bitter emotional combat with everyone around her.

She spoke of her only close friend, Judy Baum, as a friend one day and as a treacherous adversary the next. On the phone, one minute she claimed, through sobs, to miss me. The next she lashed out, her voice shaking with emotion, at my father for not sending her money, and at me for asking her for it.

After I talked with her on the phone, the momentum of growing up that I was gaining by being on my own at Bradley faded away. On the one hand, my need to talk with her out of old reflexes and also out of loneliness began to run up against my wish to be free of her. On the other hand, my struggle with her had the effect, as it always did, of making me more dependent on her the more pain my relationship with her caused me.

On the third hand ("There is always a third hand, which is what gives a mythological dimension to people, and also what makes them so prone to misunderstanding each other." —The Old Man, summer of 1977), I loved to make her laugh whenever we spoke. We shared the same impulse toward playfulness and make-believe, as well as the same deep gratification when we made other people laugh. I would mock some of my professors to her. Oh, they sound awful, she would say. Just awful.


I said goodbye to Perla and her family at the end of the summer, tearfully embracing this large Mexican woman as if she was my true mother. After my return to Bradley for my second fall semester there, I spent most of my evenings with Claire in her dorm room. I often returned to her after spending hours in the library's red-carpeted reading room. Claire had a roommate named Gabriela who would be out long enough for Claire and me to be sexually intimate. Claire and she shared bunk beds, with Gabriela sleeping in the top bunk. She didn't mind that I slept with Claire in her bed, so long as we were quiet and abstained from sex when she was there.

None of Bradley's dormitory rooms had kitchenettes, so

Claire often cooked dinner for us on a hot plate. She was a re-
sourceful cook, though she never thought anything of her culi-
nary skills, any more than she gave much thought to her other
gifts or qualities. She had been raised by her mother to think
of her own kindness, modesty, and self-effacement as being the
most admirable traits a human being could possess. This image
of herself as a good girl, implanted in her since childhood, placed
her to the side of everything that happened to her, lucky or
unlucky. Her indifference, even blindness, to achievement and
rewards protected her against disappointment when they didn't
arrive. For the same reason, her dreamy complacency prevented
her from pursuing elevated goals.

It was that angularity that she had to the world, similar to
that of Eduardo and Simon, that bound me to her. I sensed that
the retraction of her ego created ample space for me. I compli-
mented her on her chicken with broccoli, her performance in
her various classes, her lovely singing voice—she had joined the
university choir—and the diplomatic way she dealt with both
her mother and her father. She flushed slightly and laughed my
compliments away, as if self-satisfaction was both beneath and
above her. She struggled a little with her literature papers, and
as I did with Eduardo's, I took them in hand, revising and re-
writing them. To my surprise she began to ask me for my help,
a flash of ambition that I had not seen before. This was the right
kind of ambition for me since it depended on my willingness
to sustain it.

One night after dinner, Claire announced that she was going to
join some other students in her educational development class
who had formed a study group that met in a coffee shop. I had
planned to spend the night with her.

I'm sorry, she said, I promised that I'd be there.

I'll help you with your work, I said.

No, she said. It's not that kind of work. We want to expand on things we talked about in class.

You never told me about the study group before, I said.

We never had it before, she said. This is the first night.

The first night, I said.

Yes, she said, the first night.

I accused her of lying to me. After several minutes of this, she'd had enough. Get out of here, she told me. I can't take this anymore.

Stay with me, I said. I grabbed her arm.

She flung her arm away and started for the door.

Don't leave, I said.

Oh Christ, she said. Leave me alone. Just leave me alone.

Clutching my chest, I began to sob.

Gabriela had been lying in her top bunk, reading a book. She raised herself on one elbow and took us in with her large, dewy brown eyes. She said to Claire, Be careful. You are playing with fire.

I looked up at Gabriela and saw her as if for the first time. She always seemed to have come right out of the shower. Tonight she had thrown a towel over her shoulders. Her wet hair lay mostly flat on the towel, the ends of her hair tangled and askew like electrical wires that had been cut. The room was scented with the strong fragrance of her shampoo. She had dyed her hair blond but left the roots black. The contrast between her colored hair and her natural hair was disenchanting. It was as if she wanted to establish a fact about herself right up front so that she would never have to talk about it. Born in Puerto Rico, she and her parents had moved to Chicago when she was a girl, settling near Humboldt Park on the West Side, far from the Mexican neighborhood where Eduardo and his family lived. She flourished in school. Like Claire, she was studying to be a teacher.

Gabriela had a vigilant air. It was as if she had once let her guard down and was resolved not to go through the consequences of that again. When she laughed, which she seldom did, she seemed to expand and acquire a new physical aspect, like someone you have worked with for months who one evening finally comes along with you and some other coworkers to a bar, and after a few beers relaxes and shows you a different side. Mostly, though, my presence kept her alert. She maintained her distance from me.

In any case, her surprisingly sympathetic remark gave me heart. I sensed, as soon as I heard her warning to Claire, that she knew all about emotional distress and the perils of internal combustion. Perhaps on some level she thought she could handle me better than Claire was able to. I began to sob harder. I sank down onto Claire's bed with my head in my hands.

Claire had stopped at the door before opening it. She stood motionless, watching me. I had never broken down in front of her like that. Overcome with fright and self-pity, I continued to cry. At the same time, a familiar sadness enfolded me in a homelike feeling. From behind my curtain of genuine tears, I observed, with an impassive joy, how my display of emotion was magnetizing the other two people in the room.

Gabriela slipped down off her bunk and sat next to me. I raised my head and lowered my hands so that she and Claire could see the tears on my face. Gabriela put her arm around me. Out of possessiveness and perhaps competition, but also because she was moved, Claire kneeled in front of me and took my hands in hers. In a few minutes, tears filled Claire's eyes. Out of the corner of my eye I could see Gabriela wiping her own.

A gladness swelled inside me. I no longer felt frightened or sorry for myself. Suddenly, the clouds parted: I was happy and hopeful again. I was still sitting on the bed, my hands in Claire's, Gabriela's arm around my shoulders. I felt powerful, dominant, even playful.

We're like those guys raising the flag on Iwo Jima, I said. I started to laugh. Claire began to laugh also. Gabriela, though, looked at me in disapproval and withdrew her arm from around my shoulders. Either she resented me for breaking the spell of communion between the three of us, or she was made uneasy by the way I jumped from one emotion to another. But, as if unable to help herself, she started to laugh, too. The three of us laughed, then fell silent, then slowly began talking and laughing about other things. That night Claire cooked some chicken for us on the hot plate. We ate dinner together by candlelight— three candles, one for each of us, that Gabriela stuck in a small pot of soil where a plant had once grown.

After that night, the unrest between Claire and me subsided. This didn't mean that our relationship was deepening. Our relationship was coming to an end. The sometimes delicious tension of being lovers had snapped under the weight of my emotional needs. At night, we held on to each other in bed, where the sexless make-believe of being two nonhumans who had turned themselves into imaginary animals began to drive out, once and for all, the make-believe of Claire and Doug, which had always occurred right at the edge of sexlessness anyway.

Our relationship was waning not only because, thanks mostly to my vortex of need, we had fallen back into childish habits. There was a more practical reason that our relationship was doomed. Toward the end of my second year at Bradley, my mother called to tell me that my father had declared bankruptcy. He could not give her the money he was required to. As a result, she could no longer afford to pay for the room and board expenses that the student loans didn't cover. Shifting to part-time status so that I could work my way through school was out of the question. You needed to be a full-time student to be eligible for financial aid and loans, and I would not have been able to earn enough money to cover all the school expenses myself. I had to leave Bradley and return to New Jersey.

I was torn about this sudden development. I prized what little independence and small share of fortitude I thought I had won for myself by studying in an environment so different from where I had come from, and so far away from home. I felt close to Simon and Eduardo, and to their families, especially, of course, the Caravanteses. I thought that I was in love with Claire. The chief symptom of our waning relationship was that cuddling, snuggling friendship, which produced the illusion of a deepening intimacy.

But I had grown estranged from Bradley. I hungered for a cosmopolitan atmosphere electric with ideas and intellectual ambition. When I daydreamed of such a place, I imagined being surrounded by the magic that books had implanted in me, by the Old Man's reassuring detachment and long view of things, by the complicity I felt I had with the past that was embodied in books—I imagined all my secret resources being recognized and praised. I wasn't just forced from Bradley. I wanted to leave, too.


One day a political science professor I admired, and whom I often visited during his office hours, abruptly asked me: What are you doing here? You should be at a place like the University of Chicago, he said. He himself had a graduate degree from there. The next holiday weekend, Simon, Eduardo, and I set out in Eduardo's old Chrysler for Chicago. I stayed one night with Eduardo and his family, and one night with Simon and his. On Saturday the three of us drove to Hyde Park, where the University of Chicago was located.

Yet instead of inspiring me, the campus had the effect of stopping me in my tracks. A place this excellent and rare, I thought, would never allow me in.

Still, the university lodged itself in my imagination. My fantasy of the other workers at the medical book warehouse having been in prison, and my vision of what it would be like to be in prison, sprang from a feeling that had grown stronger in me: the feeling that I was imprisoned myself. The monumental limestone hardness of the University of Chicago's walls were a revelation. They were the very opposite of prison walls. They were the anti–prison walls. They kept out the forces of unfreedom: money, competition, social judgments that were all about your fitness as a social animal rather than your fitness as a human being. I might have thought that I did not deserve to dwell inside the university's sacred parameters—not yet, anyway. But the walls that made me despair of ever belonging there also inspired me with hope that I could be protected by them. Perhaps, like some humane Scandinavian country, or better yet, Switzerland in wartime—its insurmountable, custodial Alps ideally the birthright of every human being trapped in the combat of living!—I could someday find sanctuary at a university. At a great university, my fitness as a receptive, kind, creative human being—this was how I conceived of myself, for better and for worse—would finally be recognized, and my psoriatic, deluded yet irrepressible self taken under protection. I needed a university like the wonder in Hyde Park. I was sure that being a part of a community that was universally respected would have the effect of raising my own self-esteem.

Having escaped New Jersey for Bradley, I now had to escape Bradley. I loved calling Paul out of the blue, reversing the charges when his mother wasn't home. His groaning, gasping laugh made me long to continue our friendship.

I was not about to leave Claire, though. I asked her to spend the summer with me in Paramus. I still needed her, and convinced myself that we were fated to be together and that, even if I did not return to Bradley, I could live in Peoria anyway, or she could transfer to a school in New Jersey. Claire herself, accustomed to accepting things when there was an appeal to her goodness as a person, agreed to come. The world was also a strange and dangerous place for us, and the fact that we knew each other so well was a source of strength that neither of us could do without.

Together we made the nineteen-hour journey by train to New York as soon as the semester ended. From Penn Station we walked to the Port Authority Bus Terminal, our suitcases rumbling behind us as we pulled them along the crowded sidewalks. At Port Authority, we changed to a bus headed for Paramus.

# 5

# SHOWDOWN

Certain things that people said to me have stuck in my mind with the power of literature.

About twenty-five years later, in New York, after my divorce from my first wife, a much younger woman I was seeing told me a story. It was Thanksgiving night and we were on the phone. Her name was Charlotte. She had gone home to her mother's house somewhere in suburban New Jersey. I had spent the night alone, preferring to buy a takeout dinner at a delicatessen earlier in the day, which I heated up that evening, than to sit, embarrassed about having nowhere to go, in a diner or a Chinese restaurant. She had given me her number, assuming that I wouldn't call, and I took it, intending not to. In the end, I called her anyway. She was glad to have someone to relieve her boredom and to pull her away from her antagonism with her mother. I was grateful to have someone to talk to.

Her parents were divorced and she was out of touch with her father. Her mother had very little money. She lived in an affluent town in the well-appointed house the court had awarded her. Charlotte hated leaving her shared apartment in New York, where she was a graduate student at New York University, to return to her mother's house for the holiday, but she had no choice. Her mother hectored her into coming back, and threatened to stop sending her the small but vital checks she put in the mail every month if she didn't. For all that, once she arrived home, her mother, Charlotte complained, could not stop criticizing her. Infuriated by her mother, feeling trapped and infantilized, she spoke more and more rapidly, more and more half to herself and half to me, until her own voice and her critique of her mother calmed her down.

In the course of this conversation, Charlotte related to me the following story. Across the street from her mother's house, where Charlotte had grown up, there lived a couple who had once worked together in the CIA. They were married for thirty years. They raised two children who, a few years earlier, had left home to go off to college. One day, shortly before Thanksgiving, the husband got up from the kitchen table where he and his wife had eaten breakfast together every morning. He walked over to his wife and punched her in the face. He kept punching her until her face was a bloody pulp. Then, without taking anything with him, he walked out of the house and disappeared. No one had seen or heard from him since then.

Out of nowhere, my mother erupted into another person. She developed another self the way a lobster will grow another claw to replace the one that has been bitten off. I could see that these weird modes of behavior were slowly becoming normal in her eyes. She tested them at first, cautiously, the way you run your tongue over and over the hole in your mouth left by a tooth that has just been pulled. Gradually the gaping chamber in your mouth becomes as familiar as your other teeth.

Lola experimented with her new patterns of behavior as if still aware of how bizarre they were and trying to suppress them out of vanity or simply fear. But soon she surrendered herself to them.

•

My mother welcomed me back with her usual histrionics. She greeted Claire, whom she had never met before, with her customary "sweetie," "honey," and "darling," as though receiving us in her dressing room after some show. But when Claire's attention was directed elsewhere, Lola could not stop inspecting her with narrowed eyes. She made sure that I saw her as she did it.

Then, as Claire was speaking, my mother would catch my eye and mimic Claire as she talked, as if inviting me to join her, as I sometimes had done in other situations, in a show of contempt, though in this case contemptuous derision of the girl I had told her I was in love with.

Soon I began to develop ways of adjusting to her destabilizing faces—not meeting her eye, avoiding moments when the three of us would have been together, immediately starting to talk when she put on her mocking face—that made her new behavior a part of our household routine.

Angelo had not yet moved in with my mother, but he spent most evenings at her house with his children. My brother stayed locked away in his room, sorting his coins, lifting weights, and practicing his drums. He seemed to be consolidating his personal strengths and biding his time.

I had assumed that Claire and I could sleep together in my room. This was, after all, 1977, and my mother was by this point hardly unaware of the changing world around her. But she insisted that one of us sleep in my bedroom and the other in the basement, which, after many years, she and my father had succeeded in turning into another room. She was not defensively priggish like Menka, who hid his sybaritic nature behind arbitrary restrictions. It was not even that she could not bear to hear Claire and me having sex. I realized, too late, that she could not bear for us to find solace in each other in any way. I felt instinctively that Claire should stay as far away from my mother as possible, but asking her to sleep in the basement without telling her why—something I couldn't do without alarming her—was out of the question. I moved into the basement and Claire settled into my old bedroom.

Back in Paramus I had to find work. Claire, though she came from better material circumstances than I did, was in a difficult position, too. Her father gave her just enough money for her to keep turning to him for more. Her mother's finances were now almost entirely in control of her stepfather, who barely helped her out at all.

Taking the initiative, as she always did, Claire found a job at a women's clothing store called Mandee in one of the malls in town. I did not have the same good fortune. None of the people I had worked for at Alexander's or in the other stores where I had found employment were still at their old jobs. Though the country was slowly pulling out of years of deep recession—the recession that had pulled the rug out from under my father—unemployment was still high and the malls were far from lively. At Alexander's and Bamberger's, not only could I not find anyone I had known at the time I was at those places, but the personnel people informed me that they weren't hiring. When I told my mother about my problems finding a job, she stared at me, pushed her cheek out with her tongue, and nodded her head, saying, Uh-huh.

Expecting divorce to expand her freedom, she had become embittered to find that, in fact, her choices and opportunities were even more limited than they had been in her marriage. In marriage, at least, she could enjoy the daily fantasy of an emergency exit. As I later learned, a rich imagination keeps as many marriages intact as it destroys. Now, however, she was living in that once fantastical future, with new material worries, Angelo's own messy divorce, and his three kids.

A couple of weeks after we arrived, my mother convened Claire and me around the kitchen table. If I could not contribute to the household expenses, she informed me, she would not be able to afford to have both of us stay with her and Nathan. She made this declaration in a whisper, even though we were the only people there, looking only at me as she spoke, as if I was a problem that had nothing to do with Claire, and also as if Claire had no place in her house.

Claire assured her that she would happily pay for both of us out of her Mandee salary. My mother stared at her. Sweetie! she exclaimed. Honey! I will not take a single cent from you. You are a guest in my house! This of course made no sense at all. The falseness and absurdity of it drove me into the old fury.

That night, after Claire went to bed, my mother and I screamed at each other, my mother's face red and distended in lust for combat with me, and satisfaction at my disabling rage.


Angelo came to the rescue a few days later when he arrived for dinner. He had an important business connection, he said, who could find me a job in his industry. Without even asking him what it was, I told him I'd jump at the chance.

The next night he returned, announcing that he had landed me an interview with Pied Piper, a company that owned a small fleet of ice cream trucks. There's a future in that, he said. He chuckled, and then nodded to himself.

I spent the summer driving the Pied Piper truck around Paramus and the neighboring towns. At night I counted the money on the kitchen table with Claire. Sometimes my mother would come into the kitchen to look at my haul. Now, she said with a smile, you're talking.

It was a good job. Being outside pleased me and I enjoyed

the novelty of driving the tall, narrow truck that swayed when I took a corner too fast. I had a special fondness for the metal coin dispenser that I wore on my belt. It was a money-organizing machine that I mastered and controlled. The solidity of the dispenser, its heaviness as it hung from my belt, just above my groin, made me feel important, as embarrassed as I was to feel important on account of so little.

My rival was a Good Humor truck. It was operated by a Vietnam vet who had smuggled his sidearm home with him. Once he drove up beside me and displayed the pistol. He wanted to make a point. He would sometimes cut in front of me when a group of kids were beckoning to us from the street, causing them to jump onto the sidewalk.

During one of my circuits, the Good Humor driver pulled up alongside my truck. He raised his gun, a .45 semiautomatic, and aimed it at my head. He said: This is my block from now on. Okay? I had never had a real gun pointed at me before, but I was thrilled to recognize the situation from TV and the movies. I had the certainty of too much life ahead of me to believe that he would pull the trigger and kill me. Besides, a gun, which played such a pleasurable role in entertainment, could not possibly be lethal. I was a very young nineteen.


Though difficult books in literature and philosophy had strengthened my mind, I could not find a place in my emotions for what my mind had absorbed. My consciousness burst with ideas: The world is an imperfect shadow of reality. We are born free but live in chains. You cannot have an experience and reflect on that experience at the same time. Before you do anything, consider if it is the sort of thing everyone should do. When you meet a contradiction, make a distinction. Be a knight of faith and take a leap into the unknown. All the world's problems are caused by the fact that people cannot sit quietly alone in their rooms. The only question worth asking is whether you should take your own life. Live dangerously! I was a cowlicked compendium of rarefied concepts. But though I saw how my mother was trying to sever the bond between Claire and me, I still thought of her as my mother. I could not imagine that she wanted to hurt me in some fundamental way.

When I had talked with my mother on the phone from Peoria, working out the arrangements for Claire and me to stay with her, I made sure to clarify one thing. I wanted to be certain that my mother would allow me to use her Chevy Impala. By now, both Claire and I had deluded ourselves into thinking that I would return to Peoria with her and so there was no reason to find ourselves a car. I could hardly afford one, anyway. My mother agreed. She had begun teaching ESL courses over the summer to supplement her income. That, she said, was pretty much the only occasion for which she needed the Impala, and she could borrow Angelo's car in that case. If I agreed to buy groceries, I could have the Impala the rest of the time.

Almost as soon as Claire and I arrived, the Impala became a battleground.

One afternoon, I shouted upstairs to my mother that Claire and I were taking the car to go visit Paul Dolcetto. Paul and I had resumed our friendship with even more enthusiasm than before. My mother had the day off. She was lying in her bed waiting for Angelo, who was bringing his children over for dinner.

I could hear her bed creak as she slid out of it and rushed down the small staircase. We were standing at the bottom of the stairs, about to walk toward the front door.

Oh, no you're not! said my mother, grabbing the car keys that I held in my hand.

Claire froze. She looked back and forth between my mother and me. I reacted as if out of an old reflex and pulled the keys away from my mother. I had never had a physical fight with her before. During her slapping fits, I would put up my hands to protect myself and try to back away from her until she spun out of my room. But it was as if somewhere deep inside me I had been fighting with her like this all my life.

You little shit, my mother said. Her eyes were gleaming with malice. Her entire face had been transformed. It was a swollen red mask with lips stretched into a grimace that had the appearance of a smile. Obscenities flowed from her mouth. She sounded like a movie demon speaking out of someone possessed. I had never heard her curse me before, either.

You think you can do whatever you want in my house! she cried. Do you think you can fuck your little girlfriend when I'm sleeping, eh? You think I don't know what you do in the basement? When I'm trying to sleep? I need my sleep! As her rage rose into non sequiturs of self-pity, her screams became wailing shrieks.

Lola, said Claire. Lola, please.

The injustice of my mother promising to let me use the Impala and then breaking her promise enraged me. I could not allow her to take the keys away from me again. When she reached for them this time, I snatched them away.

You ungrateful little shit! she shrieked. Do you see this, Claire? she said. Do you see what the man you love is doing to his mother? He came from my body! I took care of him! I wiped him and cleaned him up. I wiped his penis. I gave him my last pennies. Everything I had! Everything! And he gives me nothing in return. Nothing! He's a bum! A bum!

The part about being a bum came from a movie that my mother had once seen and that had moved her greatly. It was called *The Eddie Cantor Story*. The scene that stayed in her mind portrayed the singer's grandmother, a saintly, self-sacrificing woman saying to him on her deathbed, when he was a little boy, "Don't be a bumma." Whenever she recalled that scene, my mother cried, and now, when she said the word "bum," her eyes filled with tears.

Lola, Lola, murmured Claire. She stared at my mother in awe.

I held the keys up in the air. My mother was blocking my path to the door, so I ran up the three steps with them. She ran after me and began slapping me on the back and on my arms.

Oh no, said Claire. Oh no, no, no, she said, running up the steps. She tried to grab my mother's hands to restrain her. My mother took hold of my shirt and then my arms. Claire struggled with my mother's arms in an effort to pry her away from me. The three of us whirled around in the narrow hallway with the pink bathroom.

My mother would not let go of me. With a long grunting sound that she made through clenched teeth, she pressed the nails of both hands into my forearm. I was wearing a short-sleeved shirt and her nails sank into my skin. Startled by the pain, I jerked the keys away from her.

She hurt you, Claire said in disbelief. My arm began to bleed. Seeing Claire gently touch my bloody arm, my mother backed against the wall.

Go, she hissed. Take the car. Leave your mother here like this, she said. My heart is beating so fast, she said. I'm dizzy. I think I'm going to pass out. Leave your mother here to die.

Pass out, I said. Die. I put the keys in my pocket and ap-plauded like a madman.

I had to get Claire out of the house. There was no telling in what direction her kindness would lead her. My mother's mal-ice flowed so obviously from her weakness that she was a double, even a triple threat.

But I did not have to worry. Claire's sensitive nature had been affronted. Embracing my arm, she walked fast with me to the door. We drove in silence on the Garden State Parkway to the apartment in Orange, twenty minutes away, where Paul was living with a roommate while attending Drew. The three of us drank wine and talked all night about what had happened in my mother's house.

For the next week, Claire went to Mandee, where she worked full-time. I drove my Pied Piper truck. My mother, penitent and refreshed, made my favorite dinners—beef Stroganoff, pot roast and kasha, chicken parmesan. None of us brought up what had happened.

At the end of the week, Claire told me that she was going home. Her father insisted on paying for a one-way plane ticket to O'Hare after she told him what had happened. It was the end of the summer and she would have left the following week anyway. We drove together to the airport. My mother lost herself in a tearful goodbye, saying, I hope I will see you again. You're part of our family now!

Claire and I promised to meet again in Peoria as soon as I saved enough money to find a place to live there. After two or three months, we stopped calling and writing to each other. I never returned to Peoria, and I never saw or heard from her again.

# 6

# SINK AND SWIM

What do you do for a living?

The immigration official had a wide face. His complexion was red from the sharp November wind. There was humanity in his broad, amiable face. I noticed that he wore a wedding band. I tried to imagine him as a father, playing with his children on the living room floor. He was a big bear of a man, with a full beard and plentiful dark curly hair. I smiled at him, hoping to strike a sympathetic chord. But he was all business. Unlike an American, he was not personally there in any part of his interaction with me. The stoniest American bureaucrat is likely to expose his personal feelings in the business he is conducting with you at some point: his refusal to yield will betray annoyance or anger; his understanding will hint at something he senses he might have in common with you. It all has to do with the great big proscenium of American life. There is so much going on, expectations are so high, reality seems so promising and gratification so impending that few people are able to remain in the audience without writing themselves into another person's life. Americans take everything personally. But duty in

this Norwegian official existed in a separate space from the rest
of him. There was nothing petulant, exasperated, or angry
about his impassivity with me. If he had seen me drowning in
the North Sea not far from his office, he would have jumped
into the icy water to save my life with the same commitment to
protocol. At least that is what I told myself to try to stay cheerful and respectful as he interrogated me.

I'm a writer, I said.

A journalist?

No. I write fiction.

If you write fiction, then you are self-employed.

No, I write fiction for a magazine.

Which magazine?

*The New Yorker* magazine.

Ah, yes. Of course. I know this magazine.

Do you?

Yes, he said. So, he asked, you are employed by *The New
Yorker* magazine?

Yes, I said. Well, not exactly.

Not exactly?

They are publishing a story of mine.

The story will be published soon?

Yes. Well, yes. Pretty soon.

Congratulations.

Thank you, sir. Thank you.

But that is one story. You need to show me that you are
receiving a salary from them. The state needs to confirm that
you will have an income while you are here in Norway.

Why?

So that you don't look for work here. The state cannot give
you a visa to work. It can only give you a temporary visa to live
here. But first you have to prove that you can support yourself
while you are in Norway without working here.

Ah, that's good. Then everything is okay. I'll get enough

money from the story to be able to stay here for a few months. After that, I'll publish another story.

The official smiled.

So much for my theory, I thought. I had touched him somehow. I smiled back. I felt relaxed and relieved.

The official continued to smile. If you were Norman Mailer, he said, laughing good-naturedly, you could stay. But you are not. So I am afraid that the state cannot give you a visa. You will have three months from your date of arrival to live in Norway. In the middle of December, you will have to return to the United States.

He stood up from behind his desk. Closing my passport with one hand, he stretched across the desk to return it to me. I got to my feet. After I took back my passport he kept his hand extended over the desk. I shook his hand. Good luck, he said.

Outside in the charming little street, I told Gretchen what the immigration official had said.

What should we do? she asked me.

I don't know, I said. It looks like we're going to have to go back.

Would that be so bad? she said.

I don't know, I said. Yes, it would be bad.

Let me see what my grandmother and my great-uncles have to say, she said.

We walked to the harbor, where we waited for the ferry to return us to Tromøy, a small island in the North Sea where we were staying with Gretchen's grandmother and one of her several Norwegian great-uncles. Ever since I had met Gretchen and she told me about her grandmother's small white house on Tromøy, the island had occupied a central place in my imagination as, finally, a new home for us, a new beginning for me, and a place to rest.

·

After Claire went back to Chicago, I had lived with reluctance in my mother's house for a few months. I had no money. Without money, I could not move in with Paul, which was my plan.

My mother resented me for having to live with her. She was waiting, with apprehension, for Angelo's divorce to come through so that he could move in. But my father was nearly indigent in his small room in Elmwood Park, a neighboring town, and she had no money to spare for me to help me move out, even if getting me out of the house served her purpose.

I didn't want to be anywhere near my mother, so I stayed in the basement. I barely recognized the person she had become. She had fallen through whatever had remained of her socialized, regulated self as if through those traps in the Vietnamese jungle with sharp wooden pikes waiting below. She was impaled on unconscious forces that most people negotiate and navigate. She was at the mercy of every absurd or ugly whim and impulse.

Two floors above me, she lay in her bed at night and listened for every sound that I might make underground. She had had another phone line installed for me there so that I could talk late at night without disturbing her. But she could not tolerate this new arrangement. Unable to sleep, I would talk for hours with Claire in the weeks after she left, or with Paul or some of my other friends. My mother would storm into the basement.

Get off the phone, she would say. I'm trying to sleep! Your mother is trying to sleep! I am so tired, she would say. Can't you see how tired I am?

From my spot on the sofa bed, I could see the dark half-moons under her eyes. She stood at the basement door, her nightgown open so that I could see her underpants and bare legs. She stood there staring at me. We were all alone at the bottom of the dark, empty house.

I'm sorry, I would say. I'm going to bed now anyway. I won't be talking anymore. Good night, Mom. She looked at me with an indescribable expression on her face—exhausted, spiteful, confused, suspicious, enraged, sorrowful, knowing, hungry, disappointed—and dragged herself back upstairs.

In fact she could not hear anything at all in the basement from her bedroom. Paul and I had tested the acoustics one afternoon when she was out. But the very thought that I was talking with a friend or with Claire tormented her.

After she returned to her bedroom, I would call Paul or Claire or another friend again, this time speaking in the softest whisper I could manage.

One night, when I was on the phone with I don't know who, I heard a click. A telephone operator came on. She told me that I had to clear the line to receive an incoming emergency call. Terrified that someone I knew had been hurt, maybe my father, I hung up the phone. In a second, it rang and I picked it up with a trembling hand.

Who is this? I cried. What's wrong? Is everything okay?

After a pause, I heard a familiar voice.

Are you trying to kill me? my mother said. Are you trying to kill your mother? Get off the phone and let me sleep. For God's sake, stop torturing me and let me sleep.


In an effort to save as much money as I could in as little time as possible, I started working at a gas station a few blocks away. My mother had pulled in there for gas one day and struck up a conversation with the woman who owned the place with her husband, and who just happened to be working the pumps. The woman explained that they were shorthanded. As my mother related to me: I informed her what a smart and talented boy you are and that you are looking for a job. That day I went over there and got hired. My mother told me how proud she was of me.

I worked a full day, pumping gas, checking oil, and cleaning windshields. The first few times someone from my high school drove in, I wanted to quit and run home before they could see me. I could not bear to witness the surprise on their faces, especially the girls'. The brief conversation that followed was usually conducted on their end in hushed tones, as if in the presence of a tragedy. After a time, I came up with a story about taking time off to write a novel before going back to school.

The story became so necessary that I began to believe it myself, and then I got caught up in it. I started to write a novel at home, at my old Ethan Allen desk late at night before going down to the basement to sleep and to conduct my surreptitious phone calls. I did not make them until I was absolutely certain that my mother was no longer awake. I knew that my mother was asleep when her bed stopped creaking and I could no longer hear her pacing around her bedroom.

Writing at night instilled in me my old sense of destiny. I began reading again, taking beloved old books off shelves of the hutch on top of my desk. I reread *The Sun Also Rises* and *Understanding the Great Philosophers.* Soon the Old Man reappeared. He assured me, once again, that one day all the world would admire me for the way I endured my ordeal.

I took my copy of Spinoza off the shelf and read to myself, over and over again this line: "All things excellent are both difficult and rare." I cherished my undercover, untested importance. I savored the ironic contrast between what I was doing and who I believed I was.

Missing the shared intimacy with literature that I had felt in my English classes at Bradley, I registered for a literature course at Bergen Community College. The classes were held not at the college, whose campus adjoined a public golf course, but in a classroom in my old high school. I tried to shrug off the shame I felt when I discovered that I would be sitting in a place that my friends had left behind, and that I also should have gone far beyond. In my eyes, the shame of it was the price I had to pay for pursuing an exceptional destiny. The Old Man provided commentary as I walked through the old corridors: "In every corner he saw traces of what he had been, and hints of what he was to become."

Despite my resolve, I was relieved to arrive at the class-room where I could feel, once again, enclosed and elevated by literature. But the class, on the eighteenth-century English novel, was nothing like what I had expected. The first novel we read was called *Clarissa*. Its heroine, who is raped by a corrupt aristocrat, suffers a nervous breakdown and eventually finds refuge with a humble shopkeeper and his wife. She dies in pen-ury. Her virtue, by dint of her suffering, is an indictment of the debased landed and moneyed class that ruined her.

The social themes were right up my alley. Most of all, the novel's affirmation of the transcendence of the human spirit above material matters restored in me that familiar feeling of having a secret complicity, by means of literary art, with fundamental truths invisible to most other human eyes.

The professor, however, a shortish woman in her early sixties with snow-white hair, took a literal approach to the book. Instead of discussing timeless themes of good versus evil, reality ver-sus appearance, robust but ultimately corrupt respectability versus the integrity involved in profound mental confusion and exhaustion —instead of taking up these worthy subjects, she in-vited into class someone from a nearby rape center, who gave us statistics on rape, first by county, then by state, and then nationally. She ended her presentation by outlining the legal def-inition of rape. The professor added that this definition applied to what had happened to Clarissa, who had been drugged and then violated. Clarissa, the professor concluded, had been a victim of date rape. She said this with a kind smile that, it seemed to me, possessed a finality of virtue that brooked no disagreement.

I was surprised by the effect the presentation had on me.

My head began to swirl with associations: the legal terminology and the sheriff's visit to our house; the leaden economic sound of statistics; the absolute moral rightness of what the two women were saying and the absolute wrongness, to my mind, of the context in which they were saying it—their moral rightness melting in my overheated conscience into the irreproachable moral platitudes on my mother's refrigerator. The class sent me right back to the place I had fled from. "There is nothing," the Old Man declared, "like a good cause to bring out the worst in people." Having not yet begun to acquire the confidence to ask questions, I was still in the declarative stage of my life.

*Clarissa* and all the other great works of literature were my alternative world above, beyond, and opposite to the filthy, transactional world that judged you by standards that didn't apply to you. My father's inability to pay back Albatross, rather than his kindness and creativity, had determined his fate. My fate, on the other hand, was being determined by higher powers. By immortal books. By immortal authors. By the Penguin Classics. I was not going to sit there and allow emissaries from the world of upside-down values—where the appearance of respectability and responsibility hid ruthless grasping and greed; where conventional standards of merit disguised contempt for true human worth—pollute the sources of my value as a person.

After the class was over, I stormed out. As I marched back down the hallways of my old high school, my rage blasted my shame to smithereens.

Once, further along in time, a black intellectual told me how food had become his enemy. His father had destroyed himself with drugs, he said. His brother, his self-esteem sucked away by the same asphyxiating circumstances, destroyed himself with alcohol. My friend said that he was determined not to be ruined in the same way. He became a great success. He avoided drugs and alcohol with religious discipline. Instead he ate, and he ate, and he ate. He tried to eat himself to death to feed his rage. One of the more toxic blends in the human mind, he told me, is success mixed with self-loathing.

I had always been angry, but for the first time I was aware of being angry. I could sit at my mother's kitchen table and eat a whole Pepperidge Farm seven-layer cake without realizing it. As I chewed, my heart pounded and my head whirred with memories of slights received. I brooded on fantasies of revenge against people who had treated me not like the boy who suffered for his offbeat merit, or the boy who could read a book like nobody's business, but like a loser who was lucky to get what he had.

I got fired from the gas station because I couldn't bring myself to quit. Remaining in a painful situation was becoming an established pattern of behavior. The minute I resolved to leave I realized that I had no one to turn to beyond the situation that had, at least, become a reliable part of my life. So I stayed put, seething to get out.

My unhappiness at the gas station had little to do with the menial nature of the work itself. In fact I was enthralled by car engines. I knew absolutely nothing about cars, or about what made them go. But I felt joy whenever I had to lift a hood and check the oil, which was all I knew how to do under a hood.

One day, however, the woman who had hired me called me stupid for fumbling with the gas hose and spilling gas over a customer's car. I told her to go fuck herself. My reaction took me by surprise. It was often like that. Inside me, I felt soft, subtle, complex, silken. But when I expressed myself in the world, through words or behavior, everything came out hard, brutal, direct, and rough.

Yet I was throbbing with her insult. So I said it again: Go fuck yourself. Then, regretting what I had said, I returned to work as if nothing had happened. About twenty minutes later, her son, who worked part-time in the office with her, tapped me gently on the arm.

You're fired, he said. Get going.

My heart sank. I hated being thrown out of the familiar, reliable world of the gas station, where I had worked for several months.

You're fired, he said again. I looked in his face for some satisfaction in saying the phrase for a second time, but he repeated it with distaste. I searched his face for compassion, but there was none of that, either. What happened in life offered you no guidance about how to proceed through it. My mother will pay you, he said.

In the office, the woman took some cash out of the desk she sat behind for most of the day. She put it in an envelope with crisp efficiency and handed the envelope to me.

You're not cut out for this kind of work, she said matter-of-factly. There was no reproach in what she said, nor could I extract any irony from it. I was not cut out for that kind of work. I wanted to feel relieved, but I was hurt.

That evening, as Nathan, my mother, and I sat eating turkey TV dinners, I told her that I'd been fired.

Wow, said Nathan. He had taken stock of the situation at home, calculated that unlike me he had several more years of having to live there with my mother, and decided to make the wedge she had been driving between us for years a permanent one.

How'd you pull that off? he said.

How did you manage to have two pimples the exact same size in the exact same spot on either side of your face? I said.

My mother pushed out her cheek with her tongue and knowingly nodded her head.

What are you going to do now, Mr. Kafka? she said. All she thought she knew about Kafka was that he was a Jewish writer who had troubled relationships with other people, especially his family. Thus she had taken to referring to me as Mr. Kafka.

I'll go back to the malls, I said. I'll see if anything has opened up.

My mother said, Audrey Castor told me that she was in Stern's the other day and she thought they were hiring.

Audrey Castor was someone my mother had met through teaching, another substitute or an administrative assistant, I don't remember. She had shown my mother some kindness. In response, my mother had obviously poured her heart out to her and this woman had obviously absolved my mother of all guilt. Audrey Castor's every word now possessed the authority of divine revelation. My mother quoted her all the time.

How would Audrey Castor know if they were hiring? I said.

How would Audrey Castor know if they were hiring? she mimicked. How would Audrey Castor know if they were hiring?

Nathan snickered. The by-product of my mother's malice was often that she could be very funny. If I started to laugh, she would laugh, too, and the two of us would share a bond once again. On this occasion I didn't laugh.

She knows people there, my mother said.

Oh, she knows people.

Don't get on your intellectual high horse with your sarcasm, Mr. Kafka. Audrey is a wise woman. And she's kind. She's lived a full life and she has a lot to teach you. To teach everyone.

Maybe she should open her own university, I said.

At least she's not a bumma. A bumma!

I'll get a job! I yelled. I'll get a job and get out of this fucking house once and for all!

Nathan snickered again.

Hey, Travis Bickle, I said. Go clean your weapon.

My mother regarded me with nodding head and protruding cheek.

You'll get out of this "fucking" house once and for all, huh? Yeah, yeah. Out of this "fucking" house. She paused and sighed. Dreamer, she said. Just like your father. A family of dreamers.

A few days later, my head pounding with scenarios of vengeance against my mother and her new guru, Audrey Castor, I drove to Stern's, a department store that was situated in the Bergen Mall, right across Route 4 from Alexander's, to apply for a job. Hatred and rage would first strengthen me, then leave me feeling naked and weak and yearning for connection. I had never worked at Stern's before, but my experience at Alexander's, Bamberger's, and Bergner's—I assumed, rightly, that Stern's would not go to the trouble of calling all the way to Peoria for a reference—made me a shoo-in for a position in the sporting goods department that had just become available.

After a couple of months at Stern's, I saved some money and felt secure enough of at least a short-term future there to move in with Paul. For all his devotion to me, he wanted to be sure that I could give him two or three months' rent up front.

Desperate to be among books again in some protected space, I also decided to enroll at Montclair State College, Angelo's alma mater, which was just a few minutes away from where Paul was living. The school had expanded from a teachers college to a general one. Angelo raved about the place he said it had evolved into. I moved in with Paul and his roommate in the late spring of 1978 and registered to begin taking classes that fall. Just over a year had passed since I'd left Bradley. Because I had deferred the payments on my loans for just a few months after my status as full-time student ended, I was still current with them and was able to easily get another small loan to pay tuition at Montclair. The tuition wasn't much, but my mother claimed to have nothing to give me. My father, from whom I was hiding in terror, was, so my mother said, living on welfare.

For the moment, I had four walls of protection: my steady income, the student loan, the university, and Paul.

The first time I saw Gretchen Anderson was in a class on nineteenth-century German philosophy. We were seated in a small classroom. Snow was falling outside the windows. I was in the row in front of her and a little off to the side. It was a frigid February morning, two or three weeks into my second semester at Montclair.

Turning to the woman sitting next to her, she said: It was so cold this morning my skin hurt! She touched her face. Her eyes grew wider as she ran her fingers down onto her neck. Suddenly she laughed. Nothing seemed to exist for her except the fact that it was cold, and that she had felt her dry skin down to her neck. Noticing that I was looking at her, she looked back as if to say: Isn't it something, the effect the cold can have on your skin! And how emotional it is making me! I could have been a lamb or a wolf and she would have given me the same look. Then she blushed, as if, her state of mind suddenly startled, she had knocked over a glass of red wine somewhere inside her that transformed her face. If it had not been for the blush, she would have seemed childlike, but after she blushed she looked down, lost for a moment in thought. I could see—I say see; now I see, or think I see, but then it was something I felt about her, or thought I felt—that there was some suppressed self-consciousness that was struggling and evolving inside her in secret. The woman kept changing places with the child. It made me want to keep looking at her. Sitting next to Gretchen, her classmate, a casual acquaintance of Gretchen's, smiled. Yes, she said. It's going to be a real snowstorm. Gretchen said: I don't believe it's going to be that bad. Then she added: At least, I hope it isn't.

At the end of class, as I was walking to the door, someone touched me on the arm. Gretchen had my book *The Philosophy of*

*G. W. Hegel* in her hand. The other woman was standing behind
her. Gretchen said: I think this is yours. Thanks, I said. That's
very thoughtful of you. The other woman giggled. I gazed at
Gretchen, who allowed my eyes to linger on hers for a second.
Then they walked out of the class.

In my midtwenties, in New York, I began going to a psychiatrist whom I would see, intermittently, for the next two decades. I ran to him in bursts of need. Years would sometimes
pass between groups of sessions. At first he charged me nothing
because I saw him under the auspices of a university community. Later, after I left the university, he charged me only what
I was able to pay him.

He was tall and gaunt, and slightly stooped. As he got up
from behind his desk, from where he conducted our sessions, he
walked me to the door at the end of most of my visits to him.
Standing at the threshold and saying goodbye, he stooped a little
more to look at me, widening one eye and narrowing the other.

His office was piled with copies of literary magazines and
intellectual journals. He himself had written a respected scholarly book about Darwin that examined the paradox of Darwin
being both an invalid and a man capable of producing volumes
of revolutionary work. His name was Ralph Colp Jr. *Colpo* means
"blow" in Italian, and Colp sounds like *culpa*, which means
"fault" in Latin. His name struck me as almost divinely ordained
for a psychiatrist, and this strengthened my belief—for which
psychoanalysis itself offers no treatment—that he was destined
to heal me.

Several of our exchanges have stayed in my mind. In one
of them, he asked me if I masturbated. Sometimes I do, I said.
Then he asked what I thought about when I masturbated.
I told him that I began by imagining kissing a woman and
undressing her as I kissed her. He asked me if thinking about

kissing her aroused me. I said that it did. He asked me if it was the most arousing part of my fantasy, even more than the sex itself. I thought for a minute and said, Yes, yes, I thought it was. It's interesting, he said, that for you kissing a woman is more arousing than having intercourse with her.

For the rest of that session, and interwoven through several more, he pushed me on this subject. I responded defensively. There was something wanting in my libido. That was the implication in his line of reasoning. I was not thrusting myself into the world. I was not taking, seizing, gratifying myself, and building on these victories toward a concrete, satisfying future. For successful, competitive, aggressive men, the kiss was the means to the goal of total physical possession. For me, the kiss was an end in itself. The pleasure every human animal owes itself was something that I, instead, deferred to the future. I preferred the promise or tease of sex in a kiss, and a kiss's emotional fulfillment.

It was true that something inside me recoiled at the thought of using another person for anything, even mutually agreed-to physical pleasure. I experienced the same heart-pounding, ATTEN-SHUN! that most humans did upon regarding another human as an object of desire. Sex preoccupied me, though the pursuit of it made me as anxious as it made me excited. It's just that it took me some time to think of another person as an animal who would, in that animal experience, require me to also be an animal. I was working so hard on my intellectual and emotional life that I could not abruptly leave it in order to gratify my senses. My senses didn't think. My senses didn't comprehend. My senses didn't console or reassure me. I had to work my way up to physical gratification. I needed to take my thoughts and emotions with me step by step—like a divorced father slowly getting his children used to his girlfriend.

For Colp the compassionate Darwinist, the septuagenarian Freudian, this was self-thwarting. It was why we spoke endlessly about my inability to earn money and, when I did manage to do so, to save or spend it wisely. He was trying to draw a parallel. I listened to him with hunger to make myself whole. Yet I had trouble following him. He made me feel that not dispatching my sexual obligations to myself in a timely fashion was somehow irresponsible. I could not really understand how all these forces of sex and money, of ambition, of moral and material consequence, could come together to either thwart or enable me.

It was also true, as I've said, that ambition appalled me. The ambition that I felt in myself beckoned me to enter the realm of social competition. There I would be judged by standard measurements of value, like everyone else. I, who prized my untested rarity and excellence, was not about to allow that to happen. As for ambition in others, it set off all my alarms. Ambitious people—ambitious for money, ambitious for professional and social status—had a nose for motion. They gravitated toward similar people who were instruments of motion. I was stuck in life, and so I turned toward the velocity of stories and ideas. You could tell, the minute I opened my mouth, that I was stuck and that all the motion in my life was in my head. Ambitious people like Claire's father looked right past me when I spoke about matters that moved me. They looked at their watches.

I began to think of ambition as a sickness. Ambitious people were too busy looking at their watches to give you the time of day. As for helping out someone who needed it: with ambitious people you could forget it. Helping out was Joey Navas's territory. He was dead as a result. Ambitious people died just as everyone else dies, but no ambitious person died, so I told myself, from helping out.

The daughter of a Holocaust survivor once wrote a repugnant essay that I cannot get out of my head. She wrote that the worst people survived the Holocaust, not the best. The animals were the ones who lived. They took food away from others, they informed on them, they beat and killed them if necessary to get their shoes and clothes, they killed or tortured someone because a guard dared them to in exchange for food or water or a chance to continue to exist. The woman who wrote the essay conceived of the life force as being fatal to life. She saw it as an obscenity that unleashed a fury to survive. In the world of the naked will to live, kindness and goodness were pathological. They led their practitioners to oblivion.

The essay itself, a product of some type of blinding rage, was obscene. Some people survived the camps because of luck. Others survived because of cunning that had nothing to do with destroying other people. The ones who did perform monstrous acts to survive often had children they wanted to live for. Or they made a calculation, unthinkable yet instinctive, that the people they killed or allowed to die in order to live themselves were going to die anyway. What was the point, therefore, of producing two corpses where there might be only one? Anyway, who could sit in judgment of people condemned to suffer in an alternate universe that is beyond human understanding? Were kindness and goodness pathological in that universe? Maybe. Passing judgment, by those outside it, on the poor souls who were trapped inside, certainly is.

Still, as I said, the essay has stayed in my mind since I read it.

The process of making prints with woodblocks is mesmerizing. You paint the wood with ink. Then you draw your picture on a piece of paper, lay the paper on the inky block, and trace the design on the paper onto the wood. After that, you carve the picture into the wood with a long, thin metal gouge to make lines. You use another type of gouge to scrape out the chips and shavings left by the first gouge. Then you mix more ink on a flat, smooth plate of glass and run a roller back and forth over it until the roller is saturated with ink. The dark ink bubbles and congeals on the clear glass until the glass also becomes dark. At last you run the ink roller over the carving you made in the wood, and you press a sheet of printing paper onto the pattern in the wood. Then you have your print.

Gretchen was studying fine arts at Montclair. The college had a first-rate department. She wanted to be a painter, but the program had her working in different media. I especially loved her prints. After we started seeing each other, I came to the studio to see her work as often as I could.

Something deep inside me thrilled to watch her work. The printmaking process was not a means to an end—to a paycheck or a commission. It was an end in itself. It was work, but it was also who Gretchen aspired to be. She was fulfilling in her work what she felt and hoped was her destiny. Like a higher power, the work organized and determined her—but only the more she applied herself to it. I sat sometimes for hours and watched her lose herself in her work late at night, after all the other students and the teachers had left.

We began to see each other regularly. Though I was still sharing an apartment with Paul, he was now in a serious relationship with a woman and he rarely slept at home. Gretchen, who was living in her parents' house about twenty minutes from Paramus and twice that distance from Paul, stayed the night at my place more and more.

One night I read to her from a book in which the author described the ancient Greeks as holding an eternal fascination because they represented the childhood of humankind. A few days later, as I sat in the studio watching her finish a print, she raised it up for me to see. It was a picture of a group of people standing around a small fire. The figures were attenuated, symbolic. A planet, sun or moon or something unknown, appeared at the top of the picture. She said she called it *The Ancients*. Handing me the piece of paper, she said, The print is for you. On the paper she had written in a large, capacious hand: "For my fine, beautiful child."

Gretchen's younger brother had drowned in a pond in the woods behind her parents' house when he was four or five and she was a few years older. The tragedy tore up her parents in opposite ways. Her father, an electrician, began to drink in quiet rage, exploding from time to time. Her mother became a nurse. According to Gretchen, who was quiet, but keen and watchful, her father surrendered to alcohol in order to press her mother into caring for him because he had lost the ability to take care of himself. Her mother, like Gretchen, was a born guardian. There are people like that. Joey Navas was like that. At night, as Gretchen passed by her parents' bedroom, whose door was sometimes left half-open in distraction, she said that she could see her father leaning against her mother as the two of them sat in bed, his head in her arms.

One night this torn, grieving man cornered Gretchen in the living room. Gretchen eventually told me the whole story. He called me a Jew-boy and declared that all I wanted was to fuck Gretchen and that, after I had fucked her as much as I liked, I would throw her out like garbage. He said it pretty much like that. He thought he was about to lose another child; he felt free to say what he believed was the ugly, unbearable truth. Her mother quieted him. At the time I shook with indignation, and with fear that Gretchen would leave me.

I saw Gretchen's father once when I came to pick up Gretchen in the crisp-looking Dodge Dart Angelo's brother-in-law had sold me for four hundred dollars. It had barely any miles on it. You need a car, he said with a broad grin, waving away my heartfelt thanks.

Two months later the Dodge stalled in the fast lane of the Garden State Parkway during the morning rush hour. Unable

to get out as the cars sped by, I sat listening to a Chopin prelude on the radio. Rush hour would be over in about forty minutes, and I thought that the traffic would thin out at that point
and I could escape. But the cars kept flying past. Now and then
I heard a screech behind me as someone braked just in time.
Then I noticed a tollbooth operator, a young black woman,
frantically waving her arms on the side of the road. I turned off
the music and rolled down my window. Get out of there! she
cried. Get out!

Opening the door, I tried to step out but nearly got hit. I
jumped back in and closed the door. She kept screaming for me
to leave the car. Breathing deeply, I slowly emerged and stood
with my back pressed to the car. Waving my hands and waiting
until a car slowed down, I gradually made it to the side of the
road, lane by lane. The tollbooth operator looked at me and
shook her head. A minute later a car drove straight into the back
of the Dodge, the first car's hood crumpling like a playing card.
The Dodge's trunk buckled, sprang open, and waved slowly in
the air. For months afterward, I had fantasies of beating Angelo's
brother-in-law to a pulp.

Sitting in the Dodge, I saw Gretchen's father open the screen
door in the front of the house and poke his head out. His fair
Swedish-American complexion reddened. It was unnerving
to see Gretchen's high color, which also rose up in her during
sex, spread across her father's face.

The sight of me must have eaten away at him because a few
nights later, he forbade Gretchen to continue seeing me. Gretchen
refused. It was the late spring, and she was standing at the front
door, about to leave the house. He slapped her face. Almost since
our first kiss, sitting on a low cliff at the edge of campus, looking
out across northern New Jersey at the Manhattan skyline that
was wavering in the distance in a haze that was now golden, now
blue, now rose colored, I had been asking her to live with me.
When she arrived that night, she told me that she would. A few

days later, her sister, two years younger, brought her things. Gretchen waited weeks to tell me that her father had struck her. Instead she drew portraits of us together, over and over, and burrowed her head into my chest as we went to sleep at night.

It is not uncommon for men to judge women quality by quality. A flaw in intellect, character, or appearance—the last usually more decisive than the first two—often means the end of male commitment. Women more often than not evaluate the whole package. If Gretchen had judged me one quality at a time, she wouldn't have stayed with me for long.

I was still aroused by the thought of a woman I loved having sex with another man. Partly this was because my emotional need for Gretchen was so powerful that its fulfillment was more gratifying than sex. As a result, I could only enjoy sex with her if I severed her from my emotions.

But mostly, the reason for my fantasy was that imagining her returning to me, and only me, from the arms of another man meant, in the irrational logic of my imagination, that I had won a victory over the world. As my desire to break into a larger life became stronger, my need to form a mental picture of Gretchen entangled in bed with someone else grew more intense. I could reenact in my head being defeated by the world and then triumphing over it.

Gretchen herself submerged my quirk into the whole world of pleasure and fulfillment that we had created for ourselves.

Shyly at first, like a boy showing his friend buried pirate's treasure, then with ardor and pride, as if revealing a secret pedigree, I introduced her to my books, and to all that I had learned from them, and to everything that I had tried to make from what I had learned. She tried to teach me how to draw. When that was unsuccessful, she introduced me to the history of art, about which I had known a little, but not much.

After a few months, we moved out of Paul's apartment. We found a place on the second floor of an old frame house in the working-class town of Passaic. The landlords, an elderly Italian couple named Pariso—just think of Paris with an *o*, they told us—informed us that they would only rent to a married couple. They reacted suspiciously when we responded that we were indeed married. But the cash for the deposit and the first month's rent, lent to us by Gretchen's bighearted nurse of a mother, was in my hand. They took the money but persisted in their suspicions, sometimes coming in and inspecting the apartment when we were out. You should clean up your bedroom, Mrs. Pariso said to us once, from her position in her rocking chair on the porch, when we arrived home in the evening.

During the day we went to Montclair State together, separated to go to our classes, then joined up again for lunch in the cafeteria or outside when the weather was pleasant. At the end of the day we met at some prearranged place. Often it was Gretchen's studio. From there we walked down the steep hill on which the college sat toward one of the levels in the vast tiered parking lot. By this point I had a new car, a used Dodge Charger, that I had bought with money saved from my job at Stern's.

I had quit my job at Stern's because it was too far away from the college and from our apartment. I also wanted to put as much distance between my mother and me as possible, though calm, unhysterical Gretchen seemed to throw my mother off balance.

With Gretchen, my mother seemed outgunned. Partly it was Gretchen's appearance that intimidated her. My first true love had long blond hair, large gray-blue eyes, fair skin, and a slightly crooked mouth. For my mother, the Jewish daughter of Russian immigrants growing up in the Bronx in the 1930s and 1940s, especially one whose aspiration to be an actress was never realized, Gretchen's living, breathing blondness and blueness belonged to the social group that inherited life's blessings, and that my mother could not relate to, or circumvent.

But the most impervious aspect of Gretchen was that she contained no piece of Lola. My mother could not work on anyone she was unable to identify with on some level. I watched her trying to maneuver with Gretchen, looking for an opening like a wrestler, smiling at her, sweetie-ing her to death, giving her absurd compliments on her flaws—You have Elizabeth Taylor's mouth, she told her. But nothing ever stuck. Inside Gretchen, the child of a Swedish American father and a Norwegian American mother, steep granite walls contained blows and disappointments. When cracks did form, from the weight of suppression, they spread slowly.

My mother, by flamboyant contrast, needed everything inside a person to be on the outside. At the end of an encounter with Gretchen, she would launch one last extravagantly insincere compliment: Sweetie, your teeth are so beautifully white! Then she would stand at the door waving goodbye, coaxing the tears from her eyes in hopes of provoking in Gretchen compassion for her, and also suspicions of her oldest son's capacity for emotional betrayal. But all Gretchen ever said was: Your mother sure cries a lot. Lola was left standing on the front steps of the split-level house, forcing a smile for all the world to see her bravely forcing it, tears streaming down her face, a gleam of wistful malice in her eyes.

It pleased me to see my mother neutralized in this way, but after Claire, I took nothing for granted and stayed as far away from Paramus as possible.

There was a ShopRite supermarket on the other side of the stockade fence that marked the edge of the Parisos' tiny backyard. Gretchen got a cashier's job there. Almost immediately she arranged for me to be hired as the person who hunts down shopping carts in the parking lot and brings them back to the front of the store.

Every now and then I swung inside and waved hello to Gretchen. Unlike me, she had been issued a full ShopRite uniform. She looked so opposite to herself that I could not resist setting my eyes on her as often as I could. I kept ducking into the store. Finally my supervisor told me that either I stayed in the parking lot and kept the shopping carts in order or I could find another job. He said this in front of Gretchen. I had no choice but to prove that I didn't just devour volumes in the Modern Library series, I belonged in them as a protagonist, too. I quit on the spot. Gretchen deliberately lost herself in ringing up a customer, but she laughed softly as I passed by on my way out.

All these humiliations, at the gas station and ShopRite, in my old high school classroom and with my mother, made me burn more and more with dedication to suffering, like a Buddhist monk on fire. I returned to Paramus's retail sanctuary and got a job in the shoe department of Herman's World of Sporting Goods in the Garden State Plaza, which described itself as one of the largest malls on the planet.

In the evenings, Gretchen cooked a quick dinner, something easy like pasta or baked chicken. Cooking held no special appeal for her. She enjoyed it because it was new and adult, a sign of her independence. Then I would read poetry to her, or a passage from a novel or a philosophical work, or she would take out her art books and show me paintings that inspired her, instructing me in how color expressed emotion, and line, intellect and order. We both took pleasure in the more or less benign power we had over each other.

At the end of the night, I put on classical music. I had been listening to it ever since, in my early teens, I discovered the record bin at Korvettes, a discount department store just down the highway from Alexander's.

Classical music served for me as a kind of superior escape from my father's beloved jazz. It also appealed to my love for the serious depths of jazz, which I listened to, against my conscious will, as much as I could.

Sharing each other's enthusiasms, we responded most passionately to Mahler. Discovering his music on the radio, I went out to buy a record and brought it home to play for Gretchen. Mahler used horns in a very dramatic and symbolic way. He liked to put them in conflict or agreement with the strings. In one of his symphonies the horns start off sounding lonely and lost, then fearful yet intrepid, then indomitable and successful, then overwhelmed by louder horns and the sinister strings. As the strings rose up to threaten the horns, I said to Gretchen, in the manner of an expert guide: That is death. She nodded gravely. When the horns triumphed in the end in a cacophonous fusion of all the instruments in the orchestra—Ta-ta!—she said, with a slight edge of admonishment: That is victory. We hugged for joy. Ta-ta! Ta-ta!

From the time we finished dinner to the time we went to bed, I was usually drunk. Since meeting Gretchen, as if in a sign of my own independence and adulthood, I had shifted from beer to red wine. I drank about a bottle a night. Gretchen, perhaps mindful of her father's weakness, limited herself to a single glass.

Stopping, bending, stretching time, the wine reinforced my sense that we had created our own self-contained world, invulnerable to the wider world's disappointments and injuries. We had no thought of anything we were doing leading to anything else. Everything for us existed in and of itself: people, experiences, works of art. Living in Passaic, studying at Montclair State, working part-time in supermarkets and shoe departments, we were living advertisements for the effects of a humanistic education: curious, contemplative, devoted to uncovering the essence of living beings, rather than what they could be exchanged for. I was convinced that you had to come from hard-pressed circumstances to believe in those lofty values enough to want to practice them. I had heard a rumor that one of the people in the Goldberg-Cohen crowd in my high school had actually written an essay about the importance of treating people as ends rather than means in order to get into Princeton. I was not so hopelessly earnest that I could not relish that, and use it to make Gretchen laugh with me at all the things I didn't know I wanted.

In the nearly two years since I'd come back from Bradley, I had not seen my father. Yet I conceived of myself as a loving son because every time I thought of him my throat thickened and my eyes stung. It hardly ever occurred to me that I was not fulfilling my obligation to him as a son. When it did, I surprised myself by sounding like my mother and complaining, in my head, that he had not fulfilled his obligations to his family.

This was a flimsy justification of the simple fact was that I still was afraid to see him. I avoided him without even thinking about whether I really wanted to see him or not, let alone whether it was the right thing to do; the way you will reflexively pull your hand away from something—a flame, a snapping dog—that is about to hurt you.

I also continued to assume that since he had once again fallen on hard times he was reluctant to see me. I told myself that this must be the case since he had rarely called me at Bradley and never tried to reach me when I was living at my mother's house. I was incapable of being honest with myself about the possibility that I was hurting him. For all I knew, his fear of being shunned by me was stronger than his desire to talk with me. And it was self-serving of me to resent him for not calling me at my mother's house. My mother had probably told him never to call. It didn't matter. The important thing was to protect myself. He would be there, I assured myself, when I grew strong and confident. At that time I would reclaim him as my father.

Gretchen never asked me anything about my father beyond what I told her. I made him out to be pitiable yet destructive to himself and to me. She nodded. She didn't need to weigh the family dynamic from which I had come. She regarded me, as she assumed I regarded her, as an autonomous being existing apart from any influence beyond the books and works of art we had chosen as our true influences. Son of Shakespeare; daughter of Monet. Even when you are in your early twenties you speculate about marriage, but the subject never came up between us. We were part of each other's life-building process, not the fruits of its completion.

Given my father's absence from my life, I was surprised when Gretchen told me, after I came home one evening from selling running shoes, that she had spoken to him on the phone. He had sounded nice, she said; not sad at all. He had asked her if she was the woman of the house. That had made her laugh. She thought I should return his call.

Her sympathy for my father stirred my own buried love for him, and I called him at the number he had left. He sounded sad to me. Maybe he was just tired, I told myself. I arranged to meet him the following evening at a diner near where he was living. He asked me to invite Gretchen, but I would have brought her anyway.


My father had put on about thirty pounds. The wreath of wavy brown hair around the expanding bald spot on the top of his head had turned white. He had on different glasses. Instead of the black frames he had always worn, his glasses were now wire. Their thinness, combined with his white hair, would have given

him an air of fragile dignity if it had not been for all the extra
weight in his face, which made him look troubled and indolent.
He was waiting for us in a booth by the window. His face bright-
ened when Gretchen, blushing, smiled at him as I introduced
them. He asked the waitress to bring him a ginger ale and a plate
of cookies. When it was my turn to order, he grew animated.

They have seven-layer cake, Lee-boy, he said. That had always been my favorite dessert.

I'll just have coffee, I said.

I could see the disappointment on his face.

Well, I said, I guess I'll have the cake. Yes, I think I'll have
the cake. The waitress seemed to shoot him a celebratory wink.
Did he, over his solitary meals, talk with her about me? When
the cake came, I lost myself in it and devoured it like a child.

Perhaps reassured by the thought that I had not drifted so far
from him after all, my father began to speak openly to Gretchen
and me. He explained that he was lucky to get his room in Elmwood Park. The room was cheap, he said, which was lucky for
him since he was barely getting by on the money earned from his
piano lessons. His trio had broken up and he was having trouble putting another one together so that he could start playing
at weddings and bar mitzvahs again. He had a few students,
but not many. Let me know if you know anyone who needs a
piano teacher, he said, looking at me and then at Gretchen. He
smiled. Gretchen put her hand on my leg under the table.

My father said: Something nice in my life. What is that?
asked Gretchen. I have a girlfriend, he said. Her name is Marcie.
That's wonderful, Gretchen said. I nodded my head. That's really
great, I said. We talk about marriage, my father said, grinning.
Oh, that's so great! said Gretchen. Yes, I said. Congratulations,
Dad. I'm glad you're with someone. But there's a problem, my
father said. She has a dog. A German shepherd. Oh, said Gretchen.
You have allergies. Like Lee. Yes, my father said. Since I was in
my teens, I have allergies. It's terrible. Five minutes in the same

room as the dog and I can't stop sneezing. I can't breathe. Oh, said Gretchen. So I told Marcie, said my father, if you don't get rid of the dog, we can't live together. Yes, said Gretchen. That's only right, I said. So of course the dog had to go, said Gretchen. No, said my father. Marcie said that the dog stays. She loves that dog, he said. But the good thing, he continued, is that she doesn't want to leave me. So that's where things stand now. Gretchen gently rubbed my leg.

We had been there for about an hour and I wanted to leave. Yet for once I did not feel threatened by my father's defeated air. The confidence Gretchen aroused in me, the feeling that I now had a life separate from his, converted what would have been a feeling of terror in his presence into a painful but manageable sadness. So as not to hurt Monroe too much, I said: We both have to get to our jobs. I wish we could stay but we'll see you soon, I promise.

I motioned to the waitress to bring the check. You're both working? my father said. I told him about Herman's, and Gretchen told him about her job at ShopRite. My father nodded. He had a thoughtful look on his face. I noticed that he hadn't asked me about school. I figured that since he was unable to help pay for it, he didn't want to bring it up.

As we waited for the waitress to bring the check, my father continued to work away at my heart. I have a special radio now, he said. It only gets the weather. I listen to it as often as I can when I'm home. I love hearing about all the different weather patterns, and about what the weather is like in different places. It was snowing in Moscow last night. Another thing I like to do, he said, is to watch the Muppets on TV. Do you ever watch them? Oh, you should. They are delightful. They help me get to sleep.

The cookies and ginger ale are my treat, I declared.

Gretchen gradually fell behind my father and me as the three of us entered the parking lot. She and I had been holding hands, and I was almost pulling her along as I walked a step or two ahead of Monroe. My confidence, it turned out, had a limited duration, like a pain reliever. It was obvious to me that, by this point, I had to get away from him regardless of his feelings. But her heart went out to him just as it went out to me. I sometimes said to her: Be more assertive, more discriminating! I didn't realize that if she had been as assertive and discriminating as I was—in constant rebellion against my essentially porous nature—she might not have stayed with me.

By the time I reached my Charger, Gretchen was standing about twenty-five feet away. I unlocked the car door and turned to face my father. Goodbye, Dad, I said. It was great to see you. I'm sorry we've been out of touch for so long. I've just been really busy with classes and work. Let's see each other again soon.

The polite words came out in a rush. His face fell. I wanted to close my eyes and open them in some other place. I could flee from my father and pretend that this caused him no pain, but I could not withstand seeing the effects of my hurting him. He stared at my impatience to leave. Then he put his hand on my arm. He looked at me without speaking. He could not bear to say my name. Finally, he said: Could I ask you something? I hate to ask you this, but do you mind? Do you have a few bucks to lend your old man? Say twenty-five dollars? He was half grinning to mask the destruction of his self-respect.

The last of my fresh new confidence ebbed away. I could have fled from him right there. Or buried my head in his chest the way I had as a child. But he could not protect me from the feeling of naked emptiness that he himself aroused in me. I had only twenty dollars in my wallet, and I gave it to him. Gretchen walked up. My father smiled at her, too shy or too ashamed to embrace her. He hung his head over the parking lot.

The two of you look like you have the world on a string, he said, looking up at Gretchen. Don't let anyone ever tell you that you don't, he said, with that grimace of a smile. Gretchen gave him her most hopeful expression, as if she knew that he was about to win the lottery. For a second, she reminded me of my father's friend, the waitress. I could see from the grateful look on his face that Gretchen's kind and hopeful smile meant as much to him as it did to me.

If American life is some sort of hundred-yard dash, whether you want it to be or not, then the true value of going to a respected college and graduating without debt gives you between twenty-five and fifty yards on everyone else.

But you cannot say this. If you do, you will traduce the beautiful idea of a meritocracy, which is that if you go to a poorly regarded school, and you work one, or two, or three jobs while you take a full load of courses; if you work until you are exhausted, sink into debt with student loans, take a year, or two, or three of extra time if you need it—then, your will almost extinguished by hard work, and worry, and distraction, your mind disheveled by academic and financial pressure; then, finally, at last, after all that, you will succeed in your wildest dreams. Unless you don't. But if there are people who do triumph in this way—and there certainly are, though many fewer than the few there used to be—no one should have to. Working out your destiny through your work is difficult enough. You should not have to nearly kill yourself simply to get to the point where you can start applying yourself to your work.

The idea of a society based on merit is inspiring. Beyond it, there is the way things actually work. There are the prisons, where the hopeless poor are warehoused; and then the community colleges, where the luckier poor and the lower middle class pay to stay out of prison; and finally the state schools, where the children of the middle class earn the brass ring of a college degree but after graduating use up the youngest, most vital part of their lives as slaves to the debt they piled onto themselves in order to go to college, unable to buy a house, start a family, or follow their talents and inclinations. They are unable, that is to say, to lay the groundwork for their own children to shift around the ladders of inherited luck that make up the beautiful idea of American meritocracy and to rise up in society themselves. That is the absurdly consequential outcome of the superficial accident of birth or circumstance, or of low confidence and a weakened will.

And if you are fortunate enough to have a gift, then not having the opportunity to attend a college where you will be taught by and study with people who are similarly gifted, a place where you will be rewarded for your gift instead of mocked or marginalized for possessing it, a place where you can come into your own intellectually, spiritually, and professionally, a place where you can meet people who will help you fulfill your destiny in your work (call it "networking" if you like)—if you are not able to find the refuge of a college or university like that, then your heart and soul will shrivel up and die.

All of this was the callow, unequivocal way I saw the world not long after the reunion with my father, when I was twenty-one.


I threw myself into my courses at Montclair, favoring literature, philosophy, and history, in that order. I also plunged into French and German. Learning another language was a revelation to me. It resembled, in a higher key, the airborne, cushiony elasticity of being drunk—as if your brain were packed in polyurethane in a box about to be mailed a long distance. Time stood still as I struggled to speak and write the foreign words. The mental reminders of my shortcomings as a person and of the limitations of my circumstances, reminders that nagged at me in English, melted away.

Learning a new language was like starting a new life, but on better terms. You acquire your native language helter-skelter, without knowing how all the pieces fit together. By the time you are able to speak it fluently, the world is already all over you in a storm of perplexity. It is a mystery what the relationship is between what you want, what you speak, and what the world is. Mastering a foreign language, on the other hand, confers on you the illusion of growing into a new world and of understanding your relationship to it, both at the same time. I savored the conversion of old words into new words, proud of my growing acquisitions of new vocabulary.

I soon discovered that I wanted different things from my experience at Montclair than most of the other students did. Like William Paterson, the college at the time was a commuter school. Its reality as a campus, a separate space away from the bustling, raucous instrumentality of the outside world, was negligible. Angelo had overstated its qualities. The students, who were mostly the sons and daughters of first-generation Americans, brought the anxious, practical demands of the outside world with them into their classes. They arrived at class, listened, took notes, turned in their papers, and took their exams in an attitude of dutiful submission. When the class was over, they disbanded with efficiency and relief. College was a means to an end: to an income that turned over the engine of adulthood. Getting lost in reflection, in questioning the way things are and how they got to be that way, was about as helpful as getting a flat tire. Culture's gray complexity was an obstacle to these students ambitious to make a better material life for themselves. There was nothing coarse or unadmirable about that. The poor are born over an abyss; working-class and lower-middle-class kids are born on a narrow plank of stability teetering on a small mountain of their parents' toiling hopes. They want more stability.

Before Montclair, working at the gas station, committed to my reading, thoughts, and ideas, I felt solitary. Here, among people who were visibly indifferent to the aspects of existence that defined me, I felt alone. Occasionally it was not indifference that I experienced but outright hostility. Answering a question in class, I spoke earnestly and at length. Some students grumbled to each other and looked at their watches just as Claire's father had done.

Of course there were exceptions to the indifference I met at Montclair. From time to time, someone would say something in class, or give a presentation that filled Gretchen and me with a special feeling of admiration and affinity. But it was hard for all of us to form a bond with each other. Perhaps it is the nature of some people who are exceptions to a social norm to feel embarrassed in each other's presence. And since almost no one lived on campus, and there were few social events that appealed to the small number of exceptions, Gretchen and I found it impossible to get close to people with whom we sensed we had something in common. On some level, we also preferred the insulated world that we had created for each other. That was why I was drifting further and further apart from my childhood friends, even Paul.

Insofar as we needed other people in that world with us, we directed our aspirations for community toward our professors. This made for some powerful attachments, especially for me, given my habit of treating my friendships and associations as all-or-nothing investments of emotion. I developed crushes on professors who I hoped might draw me up to their plane of awareness and sophistication.

Gretchen unsettled me by allowing herself to be mentored by her sculpture teacher. A lapsed Orthodox Jew, he commuted to Montclair every day from Crown Heights in Brooklyn. At his persistent behest, she modeled nude for his class twice a week. This made me hot with jealousy. No self-respecting Jewish girl would find work as a graven image, I joked to her.

Once I slipped into the side of the room when the teacher wasn't looking—no visitors were allowed—and watched Gretchen being watched by him and by the other students. Her inanimate stillness fascinated and disturbed me. Her teacher was in fact a brilliant artist, much discussed in advanced artistic circles in New York. As far as I knew, however, he did nothing for or with Gretchen except look at her. The whole arrangement angered me, mystified me, aroused me, and, on account of his so-far innocent voyeurism, instilled in me a sense of relief. Still, I hovered over Gretchen's relationship with him. She didn't mind. She needed him as the irreproachable mentor, and me as the fanatically devoted boyfriend. Years later, I found it difficult to believe that they did not become physically intimate somewhere, sometime. But perhaps he never helped her professionally because she refused to give him the intimacy that he wanted. Neither Gretchen nor I ever brought the subject up. It was too far from the safely circumscribed world we had created for ourselves. And her teacher was too much of an actual threat for me to make him part of my fantasy.

As for me, an "A" scrawled on the first page of a paper or on an exam suffused me with faith in the future. Gradually the Old Man's voice began to fade away. He was being replaced with confirmation of the rich, sensitive, cultivated person I had always hoped I was.

One or two professors at Montclair resented their lowly academic status, expressing their frustration by elevating mediocre students and harshly evaluating anyone with talent. For the most part, though, the people who taught there were grateful to find students drawn to the fields they had chosen to spend their lives working in. They responded with generosity to my ardor, and particularly to the oblique way I had of looking at things.

You use big, Latinate words, an Indian professor of classics said to me with a kind smile; they are as big as your ambition. Keep your ambition big, she said, but use smaller, Anglo-Saxon

words. I was in the class she taught on Virgil's *Aeneid* in English
translation. I cherished the book's theme of "the tears in things."
The image of the hero Aeneas carrying his aged father on his
back out of burning Rome riveted me.

Her remark about my vocabulary at first had a crushing
effect, especially coming as it did from a professor of Latin, of
all things. One of the articles of faith that kept me going then
was my conviction that I had an absolute command of the
English language. There was also her use of the word "ambition."
As always, it made me feel stripped of my singularity; and it
exposed my embarrassed ambition. After a while, though, getting into the practice of making a conversion like "teary-eyed"
for "lachrymose"—one of my favorites—began to liberate me.
It was as if I was finding within my native language a new foreign language that was closer to how I really thought.

While Gretchen had the Orthodox Jewish sculptor, I found my
own mentor. David Einman, a professor of French and German,
was in his early sixties. I had taken his course in intermediate
French. Born in Brooklyn, he was short, bespectacled, soft-spoken,
and wry.

Einman had an almost perfect dome of a bald head. Upon
encountering him for the first time, you had no real impression
of him, so predictably did his mild aspect seem to follow from
his appearance. He did not reveal himself as a distinct personality until he removed his thick, obscuring bifocals. He did this
from time to time to rub his eyes. They were light blue. As he
rubbed them into a watery redness, carefully, with the backs of
his bent fingers—he was fastidious about himself—you glimpsed
a hidden steeliness.

Einman often surprised me by being balanced and objective where I expected—wanted—him to lose himself in some
impassioned bias that I could share. He could also be unsparing

in his mild way. What are you doing here? he asked me once, as we sat in a Montclair diner, drinking coffee after returning from a studio concert at WQXR, a classical music station once owned by *The New York Times*. The concerts were free, as I remember. Einman loved them. It made him happy to bring me along.

You invited me, I said.

No, he said. At Montclair State College.

I don't know what you mean, I said defensively.

You should be in a more intellectually challenging place, he said.

*Vous êtes très gentil*, I murmured. My shame at feeling like a failure now gave way to my usual embarrassment at the thought that I might be a success. Then I exclaimed: That's why I deserve to be in your class!

People who said kind things to me made me so grateful that I could not restrain myself from flattering them extravagantly— sweetie! honey!—in return. Einman moved his mouth and eyes to one side in an expression of exasperated incredulity, as if to say, "Well, we know *that*'s not true!"

I can give you some of what you need, he said, but not what you fundamentally need. He had the clear-eyed, rational soul of a French intellectual. I admired him for being able to correct the circumstances of his birth, and to remake himself in the place where he belonged.

I need people to tell me all the things I don't know, I said. I need people to lead me to truthful things, and to beautiful things.

I lowered my eyes. I had meant to respond with all the wit and sophistication I believed I had in my head, and out came these undistilled thoughts straight from my heart.

There are people here who can do that, he said. Of course there are. But you need to be challenged more than you are here. And you need to be someplace where the degree is worth something. Somewhere that puts a higher value on your talents. A college that is valued more highly by the people you are going to need to help you.

Like where?

How about Columbia? Einman had gotten a degree in music from Columbia.

I was thinking, actually, of leaving school completely and becoming a writer, I said.

Einman looked at me.

That's a hard life, he said. Better to get your degree and then go on and get a graduate degree and find a teaching job. Transfer to a better college. That way you can get into a good graduate school. From there you can get a teaching job at a good place.

What about my writing?

Then you can write.

With the exception of Gretchen, I had not told anyone about my plan to write. Gretchen thought it was a brave idea.


After our coffee, we got into Einman's ancient Volvo. He was going to take me back to my apartment, but first we had to stop at his son's apartment and drop off some items he had bought for him at the grocery store earlier in the day.

The product of Einman's first and only marriage, which ended in divorce, the son, Adam, lived by himself in Bloomfield in a garden apartment not far from Einman's own modest apartment. Although in his midthirties, Adam was unable to take care of himself. Einman had told me about him, but this was the first time I had met him.

At first, aside from his unkempt appearance, you could not see anything more than a little eccentric about Adam. He put you in mind of a nineteenth-century Russian revolutionary. He had nervous dark eyes and unruly matted hair, and a beard down to his chest. He wore blue overalls, a flannel shirt, and tan work boots. This made him look like Solzhenitsyn living in Vermont. Einman had told me that he never changed his clothes.

Adam talked in a high, querulous voice, almost singsong, as if, while he was searching for a way back to the theater after wandering offstage during his performance in an opera, his voice had lost its magical humanity. He had a compulsion to criticize and rebut everything that was said to him. When Einman introduced me as his student, he sneered. When his father told him that we had been to a concert in the city, he said that live concerts depressed him. Recorded sound was superior, he scolded, though still corrupted by technology. All the while he sneered as he talked. At the same time, he repeatedly asked me if I was comfortable. He brought me a glass of water. Then he asked me if it was the right temperature. Before I could answer him, he explained that I should not drink too much of it because the level of toxins in New Jersey tap water was unusually high.

As his father went out to the car to bring in the groceries, Adam invited me into his room. Old editions of *The New York Times* were stacked against every wall to the ceiling. Adam continued to talk, jumping from one subject to another: politics, baseball, music, architecture. Behind his compulsive, hypercritical commentary, underneath his perpetual sneer, his anxious dark eyes appealed to me to understand him. I shuddered as a picture of him began to form in my mind. He was not a Russian revolutionary or a Russian dissident in exile. He was Dostoyevsky's Underground Man! Two plus two equals five. Lucidity is a great disease. Madness and suffering are the price you pay for a special destiny. He kept sneering as he talked, while his eyes persisted in trying to draw my sympathy. I recognized the sneer: I had seen it on the faces of homeless people in New York, that knowing sneer that harbored the fantasy of a superior secret and which struck such terror in me. These people, sitting or lying on the sidewalk, pressed against the side of a building, also found refuge in the newspapers. They covered themselves with pages of *The New York Times* or the *Daily News* or the *Post* as they slept. I found it cruelly ironic that people so hurt by the cold, hard facts of life could seek protection underneath them. Perhaps they felt reduced to a cold, hard fact themselves. Or they instinctively felt that the newspaper's rational organization of the facts would shelter them. The homeless and their rituals disturbed me.

Gently telling Adam how much I liked his room, I went out to the living room, where Einman was playing a passage from the Mahler symphony he knew I loved, on the baby grand piano he kept in his son's apartment.

When the next semester began, in the fall of 1979, I didn't register. Like extracting a pearl from an oyster, I took to heart Einman's encouraging words and discarded his warning about trying to succeed without a college degree. I could not imagine getting into Columbia, or being able to afford the tuition if I did.

Life as a writer was not what I expected. I knew no other writers. I knew no writing teachers or editors. I had to draw every last bit of strength from the exalted notions I nursed about myself. Taking on more hours at Herman's while Gretchen finished up her degree and worked as a waitress at an upscale restaurant in Montclair, I spent my spare time writing stories. I had sent out about a dozen of them, by this point to various magazines, with no luck. I just needed more time, I told myself. Meanwhile, my job at Herman's was becoming untenable. I had a new boss who openly indulged some sort of irrational dislike of me. He insisted I work overtime for no additional pay. When I protested, he threatened to fire me. I finally asked him why he was pressing me to work more hours. Because, he said, you are my stupid cunt.

That night Gretchen and I went over our budget and decided that we had enough money in our checking account—we
had no savings account—for me to quit if I could find another
job in three weeks. Because of my reluctance to walk away from
any situation that had become familiar, it took me two weeks
before I could bring myself to leave Herman's. One week later,
I had patched together enough part-time jobs in the malls to
help keep us going.

I worked on my writing at odd hours, depending on my
schedule. The work went very slowly. Sitting outside on a bench
at the Garden State Plaza during my lunch hour, I watched the
people pass by and composed page after page in my head about
who they were, where they were going, and what they were
thinking. Driving home on the Garden State Parkway, listening
to WQXR, I could barely suppress my excitement at the images
unfolding through my mind. The expressive music enlarged and
animated my thoughts. But when I got home and sat in the
kitchen at the old card table that I used for a desk, I could think
of nothing to say.

After some months of this, I began putting the writing off.
Instead I drank wine at night and listened to music as I enacted
my stories in my head. I told myself that I needed to develop
them before I set them down on paper. For a while this restored
my confidence. In my head my stories seemed to find their proper
dimensions. I kept them there, untested, waiting to ripen and
mature. As a sort of interim exercise, I worked on my style.
Sometimes I would spend an entire week describing the sunlight
as it seemed to sweep the shadows across the street against the
curb. Gretchen showed me a book of paintings that Monet had
done of the facade of a cathedral at different times of day. I told
her that I wanted to try that in prose. The idea excited her, she
said. We affirmed ourselves through each other's attempts at
self-expression; the more quixotic or eccentric or even futile such
attempts seemed, the more gratified we were that our emotional

services would be required when it became clear to one of us that the other's efforts were leading nowhere. To strengthen my confidence I read constantly. Reading established in me a sense of my own power and intelligence. I began to think that reading had something to do with my special destiny.

Retail was losing its enchantment. Working in the sporting goods, men's furnishings, and housewares departments of three different stores drained my energy. I began to eat more, as if taking my revenge on a world that was consuming me by day by consuming pieces of the world at night. On my way home I would buy a package of salami and a container of potato salad. Sitting in bed and reading, I dipped the salami in the potato salad and washed the food down with red wine. I continued to read, work my stories out in my head, and practice my style, certain as ever that my talents would be recognized in the end. But beneath my conscious existence my life was moving in a different direction.

One morning I decided that I would sleep a little later rather than wake up to read or write before going to my job in the afternoon. The next day I did the same. Then I began going to sleep in the late afternoon after coming back from working the early shift. This went on for some weeks when, sitting at dinner one evening at the kitchen table with Gretchen, I began to cry and did not stop crying until the next morning. I dragged myself off to work and upon arriving home that afternoon made my way straight to bed. This pattern repeated itself for many weeks.

My mother's cousin Hyman had helped her hang on to the house. He was a high-priced divorce lawyer in New York who had advised my mother free of charge. Weary irony about what he did for a living was one of the perks of his success. He could be sincere, too, and ardent. He had contributed ten thousand dollars to the political campaign of Ramsey Clark, a former

U.S. attorney general who was running for senator from New York on a platform that mostly consisted of calling for an immediate withdrawal from Vietnam. Helping out Clark meant a great deal to Hyman, and he referred to it whenever he visited us. Then he would lapse back into weary, worldly irony, as if to maintain his balance, and tell another story. As a young lawyer, he had gone to visit Judy Garland, who was a client. When he arrived at her hotel suite, she was lying on the sofa, incapacitated by drugs and alcohol. In the half-darkened room, he at first mistook her for a pile of clothes, he said. My mother's eyes widened every time she heard the anecdote. Hyman told that story many times.

A cultivated man, with an offhand philosophical attitude toward life, Hyman engaged me in talk about books and writers when he came to visit. I was in my early teens. When I told him of my growing love for classical music, he made sure to ask me what I was listening to. He was a great teaser. Once he asked me what composer I loved most. Rachmaninoff, I said solemnly. Rachmaninoff! he said, shaking his head. Schmaltz, he said. Good for cooking. How about Brahms? he said. Oh yes, I said. Brahms. Brahms is incredible. He sighed. Brahms is Beethoven continued, he said. Brahms wrote strictly to make his mother proud. What do you think of Beethoven? Well, I said. It all starts there, doesn't it? He shook his head again and laughed. Bach, he said. He's the one. He married reason and emotion. Someday you'll know what I mean. Right, Monny? he asked my father. My father could have written the history of jazz in musical notation, but he knew nothing about classical music. Isn't Bach the heppest cat of all? Hyman asked. My mother, who had been listening to the exchange, laughed and sat down next to him on the green silk sofa. Hy, she said, laughing and patting his leg.

I decided to write Hyman a letter asking him to help me find a job in book publishing or at a magazine. According to my mother, he was well connected in New York. I figured his friends were all like him, cultivated people with a strong intellectual bent who would respond to my passion for art and literature.

I also asked him for a loan that could tide me over for a year until I started the job. I felt certain that if I could have a year of freedom, I would achieve a breakthrough with my writing.

I had no hesitation about asking him to lend me money. I had borrowed money from Paul, and then from Eduardo, Simon, and Claire. Perla had lent me money, along with giving it to me. Eventually I paid them all back. A feeling had grown in me that since I was living along a different trajectory than other people, I possessed an exceptional status that made borrowing money a natural extension of the life I had chosen for myself.

I didn't think the world owed me a living; not at all. Somewhere inside me I felt that borrowing money, which I would return down the road, was a legitimate form of income. It was money in exchange for the development of a talent-in-progress that one day would establish a place for me in the world. The nature of this income in the form of debt corresponded to the nature of my secret rite of passage. Both had to wait for the future to be fulfilled. In the lengthy gestation of my talent, I was borrowing against my youth. In the acceptance of money loaned to me, I was borrowing against the equity of my talent.

I sat down at the used Smith-Corona I had bought for myself at a small typewriter store on Bloomfield Avenue in Montclair and wrote Hyman a letter. My aim was to convince him that I was a good investment. Beginning with Plato and Aristotle, I worked my way up to the present day, weaving ideas and historical events together in order to demonstrate the effect each had on the other. I included everything I thought I knew. The mastery and power that I felt as I was writing transported me. I had experienced nothing like that when I was trying to write fiction. Perhaps this was what I was cut out for, I thought. To bring all the strands of knowledge and action together so that I could explain the world to other people. By the time I finished I was ecstatic. I had dispelled all of my doubts about myself. The letter was twenty-five pages long. I carefully sealed it in a large manila envelope, bounded off to the post office, and sent it to Hyman at his office in Manhattan.

Two months later Hyman's reply arrived in the mail. It was four sentences. In the first sentence, Hyman thanked me for writing to him. In the second, he said that he knew someone who owned a restaurant near Montclair who was looking for a bus-boy, and that I should call Hyman's secretary for the number. In the third, he informed me that he was enclosing a check for two hundred dollars. Then he wished me luck.

The letter knocked me out for a couple of days. I called in sick to my several jobs and stayed in bed. Gretchen cheered me by framing *The Ancients* and hanging it in our bedroom. Finally I roused myself through my trusty boosters of hatred and con-tempt. I sat down and wrote Hyman a terse response: "I am more concerned about lawyers' fees / Than American involvement overseas." Though I never sent it to him, the act of dismissing him in words steadied me.

I deposited the check and told myself, to my great satisfac-tion, that I would never pay him back.


Gretchen and I had been toying with a plan B in a vague yet persistent way from the very beginning of our relationship. We thought we might like to live in another country. I believed that a new environment and new people in my life would aid me in the construction of a new self. I no longer drew strength from my friends. With them, I was still the same old Lee Siegel, clowning around, riffing on my encounters with art and ideas, trying to make people feel good about themselves the way I needed them to make me feel good about myself—until some-one failed to respond to my distress signals, in which case I savaged the traitor to Gretchen, who listened with a mixture of solidarity and pity for me. Because I was closest to Paul, my friendship with him began to suffer the most. The more I drew on his emotional sustenance, and the more loyally he responded, the more a part of me recoiled from the familiar way he related to me. Couldn't he see how I was evolving?

Lacking a clear sense of how she was going to pursue her art after graduation, Gretchen shared my impatience to flee. Painter that she was, she found a more distinct shape to her future in the imaginative clarity of a faraway place than in the dreary familiar form of her life. School and work, school and work, with no line out of either to a larger existence, were becoming more oppressive for her every day. She also wanted to deal a blow to her father, who had refused to talk to her since she and I started to live together in Passaic.

Gretchen did not at first present Norway as a possibility. Though her grandmother was her mother's mother, asking her to allow us to stay with her while we established ourselves there would have brought Gretchen into direct conflict with her father, whom she feared all the more for defying him. Seeing her hesitation, I did not bring Norway up.

Instead I hit on my own idea: Israel! Until that moment, I had not given a thought to my Jewish background since my low-key bar mitzvah. I was not even sure what Zionism meant, exactly. Of course I rooted for Israel in the country's conflicts with its neighbors. Israel was the home team. But no one in my family had ever been to Israel. The idea of finding a spiritual home there was something that I had never considered.

My closeness to Judaism mostly consisted of the sickbed obsession with the Holocaust I had when I was a child. Images of its atrocities were inscribed in my mind. It struck at the core of my identity to conceive of Judaism as a religion that had to go underground for centuries, nursing a secret destiny, only to reemerge and be brought to the brink of extinction in Nazi Europe. I thought of Judaism as another of those big, mighty-seeming entities that were actually vulnerable and exposed. The idea of Judaism as a positive spiritual and ethical system of values never occurred to me. I had read, however, that all Jews were welcome in the Promised Land, where they automatically became citizens. Gretchen and I began reading up on Zionism, the history of Israel, and the structure of a kibbutz.

Within two weeks, after heated immersion in one volume after another on Jewish theology, history, literature, and religion, after excited nights discussing Theodor Herzl and Ahad Ha'am and Gershom Scholem, after drawing up but never executing my plan to introduce myself to the famous liberal rabbi and intellectual Arthur Hertzberg, who I discovered led a congregation in nearby Teaneck—after this excited labor the upshot was that nothing affected us so much as Eva Marie Saint and Paul Newman in *Exodus*, which happened to be on television one night. Its vaguely Mahler-like musical score was the final touch.

We visited the Israeli consulate in New York. Once through security, I walked in with a mixture of wariness and high expectation, like the prodigal son. Gretchen walked shyly as close behind me as she could. When the consular official, a woman, informed us that in order to be eligible for citizenship, we would have to marry and that Gretchen would have to convert, Gretchen looked at me for clarification. I protested the absurdity and the heartlessness of it. The woman, sincerely apologetic and harried, stuffed some brochures into our hands and looked with sympathy at Gretchen. Convert and come back, darling, she said. There will be a place for you in Israel.

It was all too much for me to consider. I wanted to live in Israel to become me, not to become a son of Zion. I left disgusted with this disappointing outcome of six thousand years of Jewish history. Now the entire religion seemed to me to resemble those ambitious people I feared and disdained, who had no space or time for me. As for Gretchen, she seemed relieved.

We then went to the Italian consulate, an unsuccessful effort for which we had read Dante and a book written in the nineteenth century called *The Civilization of the Renaissance in Italy*, followed by a visit to the French consulate, where my quoting Stendhal to the official in his native language had no effect. Finally, I abandoned my tiny store of discretion and pressed Gretchen to test the prospect of Norway with her mother. For Gretchen's mother, the fact that her daughter seemed happy outweighed every argument against me. She urged Gretchen to write to Norway. Now in her eighties, Gretchen's grandmother wrote back promptly with joy. She warned us that she could do nothing to make our stay in Norway permanent, but that she would be happy to let us live with her while we tried to make a life there.

The Parisos had finally had enough of our untidiness and asked us to leave. We moved to a small two-room place in a grand old apartment building in Montclair. In the winter of 1980, when I was twenty-two, as we were starting to make our rounds to the various consulates, Menka died. I had not seen him as much as I had when I was living in my mother's house after coming back from Bradley. But despite his anger over my mother's decision to leave my father, they had remained close, and my mother still made regular trips into the Bronx to bring Menka and Rose to Paramus for the day. I often came to visit with Gretchen when I knew he was going to be there.

Whenever my brother or I alluded to my father, Menka shook his head and sighed. I interpreted this not as contempt but as a general sadness about my father's fate. I could not endure the thought that Menka shared my mother's antipathy toward my father. Menka occupied too special a place in my emotions. He was my grandfather. My Papa. Where my parents had flaws, he had inexplicable attributes. As I grew up, I could understand, or thought I understood, reasons for my parents' behavior. But what Menka said and did started and stopped with Menka. The cause of my mother could have no cause himself.

A small group of people had come to the funeral chapel on the Upper West Side where Menka's body lay for viewing in an open coffin. Now married to a practicing Catholic, my mother had insisted to the Reform rabbi, a sympathetic man who had known our family for many years during our loose affiliation with his synagogue, on embalmment and viewing of the body, two exceptions to Jewish tradition.

To my amazement, my mother was subdued. The situation had put her at center stage. Because people already pitied her for her loss, she did not have to attract attention to her grief through an emotional display. She could begin a new relationship with Rose, too, squatting in front of the chair Rose was sitting in and speaking softly to her. She was no longer in the tormented position of having to compete for Menka's affection with the one person who had always defended her to Menka.

Hyman was in the small crowd of people at the chapel. He acknowledged me with a slight nod of his head and began to walk over to me. Hyman, I whispered to Gretchen. She had never seen him. Talk to him! she said. No, I snapped, and turned my back. I wanted desperately to talk with him, but I was afraid that if I surrendered my hatred of him, I would be giving up the fire of resilience that his letter had stoked in me. It was his letter, after all, that had made me resolve to go to Norway to start a new life. Gretchen started to walk toward him, but I placed my hand on her arm. She turned to look at me. She fixed her eyes on me and seemed about to say something. But then she stood beside me.

My brother came over to us from the coffin, his face

transfixed with horror. He shrank! he said. My heart plunged. Death terrified me. I had never seen a dead person before. Forcing myself toward the coffin, I stood alongside it, peering in. Nathan was right. Menka had shrunk. He had become an object, a thing. I did not know what to think. People are not things. You are not prepared for when a person becomes a thing. I did not know what to think, and I could not understand what I was feeling. The empty residue of his life lying in the narrow box repelled me. I loved him. I wanted to touch him. But I could not touch It. As a child, I had been tempted to touch Menka's swarthy, wrinkled hands as we played his favorite game, gin rummy, for hours, but I was afraid to. Why had I been so afraid to touch him when I was a child? I stretched out my hand. My brother whispered in my ear: No, don't! You'll push his face in! My mother stepped between us. They did a beautiful job, she said, wiping tears from her face. Look at the job they did. She slowly nodded her head. Yeah, yeah, she sighed. Yeah, yeah.

Gretchen graduated from Montclair in May, and we arranged to travel to Norway in September. We hoped that would give us enough time to save money for the trip. We mostly needed money for the journey there—plane tickets to London, train tickets to Newcastle, and then passage on a boat across the North Sea to Kristiansand. Once in Kristiansand we planned to catch a bus to Arendal, a small town on Norway's southern coast, about five hours by train south of Oslo. A ferry ran from Arendal to Tromøy. There, at Gretchen's grandmother's house, we could live cheaply, buying and cooking our own food. Her grandmother had written to us again, telling us that she had already set a room aside for us.

   The lease on our apartment was up in June. Paul, who was now living with his girlfriend, another student at Drew, offered to let us stay with him until September. We sold our furniture and put the rest of our possessions in a small storage locker that we rented in Passaic. The exception was the stories I had written and the writing exercises I had done. Both ran to hundreds of pages. I could not bear the thought of leaving them in the tomb-like storage locker. I packed them carefully in a large box and called my mother to ask if I could leave them with her along with the box of stories I had tucked away in the basement before going off to Bradley. Some deep part of me still turned to the house where I had grown up. By now Angelo had moved in with his three children, but my mother promised to find a place for my stories. When I arrived with the box, however, her mood had changed. There was no space, she said, throwing a reproachful look at Angelo, who was sitting beside her at the kitchen table, where we were talking. He waved his hand in the air in order to amiably exonerate himself from my mother's charge of his complicity in my exclusion. I'll make room in the garage, he said. He did not want to be the cause of any more friction between my mother and me. He said that he had found the box of stories I had left in the basement, and that he would put those in the larger box, too.

Our stay with Paul began well. Despite my growing disenchantment with the way my reliance on him tugged me back to my old life, in recent weeks our friendship had reached a peak of mutual sustenance. After I came home from work, he and I would drink, talk, and listen to music until well after midnight. His girlfriend, Marisa, would call to him from the bedroom to come in. In a minute, he would call back, winking at me. But one night in the middle of the summer, he got choked up.

You're going to have to leave, he said. He nodded to the bedroom. I want you to stay, he said, you know that, man, but I have to keep the peace. He grunted. He had started grunting in stressful situations a few years earlier, around the time he stopped getting nosebleeds.

I laughed out of the old habit of attachment to him. I'll talk to her, I said.

No, he said sternly. No is no.

He had never spoken to me like that before. Paul had a low tolerance both for being pushed around and for trouble in his life. Besides that, he was protecting his future.

We moved in with Terry Cushman, another friend I had kept up with since returning from Bradley. I had not been nearly as close to Terry as to Paul. In fact I had never really trusted him enough to think of him as a close friend because of the derision at the heart of his laughter whenever I made one of my jokes. But his distance from me existed side by side with his reliability. He was always ready with some kind of practical assistance, whether it was to pick me up when my car broke down or to meet me after one of my crippling fights with my mother for a heart-to-heart talk that never went very deep. He was happy to put us up for a couple of months before we left for Norway.


Does the gambler who keeps losing continue to gamble because he wants to keep losing? Does the woman who repeatedly gets involved with men who hurt her do so because she wants to be hurt? Does the man in over his head financially keep borrowing because he secretly wants to put himself in the power of other people? Was the real reason I wanted Gretchen to have sex with another man that I thought I didn't deserve to be with her? Is everything you do that leads you into unhappiness the result of some dark thing that you want that lurks beneath everything you think you want? Or are our mistakes of unhappiness simply misjudgments, cognitive stumbles? Do we want the wrong things, no matter how painful they are when we get them, because we were aiming for something else but missed? Because this was the only way we knew how to try to get the right things? Because given the information that we have, and the character that we possess, and the conflicting desires that tear at us, this is the only way we know how to keep going toward happiness?

From the beginning, the sex Gretchen and I had was filled with emotion. This was the way I liked it. We would begin tenderly, and then proceed, becoming freer with each other as we grew to know each other. After we had been together for a while, our personalities started to dominate our sexual relations. Gretchen took as much pleasure for herself as she could quietly and deeply, while I tried to satisfy myself greedily, hungrily, as quickly as possible. To the extent that some degree of the old tender intimacy remained, Gretchen enjoyed herself the more she came to know me. For me, however, the opposite was true, as had always been the case with me. Though I required emotional intimacy to become aroused, I needed to burst the emotional intimacy to stay aroused. This was where the fantasy of the other man came in. I could take deep pleasure in this sexual fantasy that hovered in a phantasmal future and that would never be fulfilled.

At Paul's apartment, and then at Terry's, it was different. Perhaps it was because we had lost the safely enclosed home of our apartment. Out in the world, with no fixed place to live, we saw each other with fresh eyes, and with a kind of urgency, and this had the result of making me more open to what she wanted. Another man was the last thing in her mind. What she wanted was her own pleasure flowing out of the relationship with me. Now, at Terry's, I kissed her and touched her until she asked to have me inside her. I loved to make her shudder in my arms and to kiss her ice-cold mouth. It was wondrous and strange to me that all the physical heat we created in each other made her shudder and grow cold. It was like some mysterious contradiction echoing out of the distant future, when thirty years later I witnessed my wife laboring in agony for the joy of making a child. In gratitude for my tender shoot of self-surrender, Gretchen threw herself into pleasing me.

One hot August evening, as we sat drinking with Terry at a table in a bar, I urged her to kiss him. She was wearing a short summer dress and clogs. I had had two or three glasses of wine. My head began to pound. Terry stared at me in alarm. Gretchen looked at me in surprise. When I said it again, her eyes narrowed. They both leaned forward, laughing slightly in embarrassment, and clumsily kissed. They stopped kissing and gazed at each other. Then, without looking at me, they kissed again.

We went back to Terry's bedroom in his apartment and took off our clothes. I watched her and Terry fuck. Then she and I fucked. Out of the corner of my eye, I saw Terry leave the room and heard him urinating in the bathroom. He came back and we all drank some more wine. Everything became a blur. He began to throw her around in the bed as she laughed, her hair flying. She looked like a doll, a thing, getting tossed around and bouncing up and down on top of him. I was both horrified and aroused. In the middle of it she turned to look at me. She had hatred in her eyes. She began to fuck him harder, driving herself onto him. I could see that she hated me for making a harmless fantasy come true.

When we were all done, Gretchen and I walked back to the room we were staying in at the other end of the apartment. Once we were in bed, I asked her if she still loved me. No, I don't, she said. I began to cry. She put her arms around me and pressed my head onto her breast. I love you, she said. Two weeks later we were on the plane on our journey to Norway. We never spoke about that night again. But the fantasy of the other man resurfaced after a while, and stayed with us.

●

In preparation for what we hoped would be our new lives in Norway, I had packed as many of my precious books as I could into a large, light blue Samsonite suitcase. The airline boarding agents weighed the suitcase at the airport: it came to seventy pounds. It was as if I wanted to entirely replace my old life with what I hoped would be the most dynamic contents of my new life. By the time we got to the house belonging to Elsa, Gretchen's grandmother, the weight of my new existence had caused me to pull a muscle in my right arm and had nearly given me a hernia.

On the bus ride north toward Arendal along the coastline from Kristiansand, I marveled at the landscape. It was not the unfamiliar elements of it that aroused wonder in me—the rising and falling craggy edge of land, the choppy North Sea lying gray under the September sky. What entranced me was the way the sky and trees, aspects of the physical world that I had seen all my life, suddenly acquired an air of mystery. The sky and trees I was gazing at were someone else's sky and trees. They seemed hidden behind eons of being looked at by people who spoke a different language and practiced different customs. I was thrilled by this alienation from the new world I was inhabiting. It meant that I could not easily understand the people who lived in it and that they could not easily understand me. It provided me with an opening toward starting over again in a place that had not made up its mind about me.

Elsa did not speak more than a few words of English. Her brother Lars and his wife, Anna, could slowly piece together rudimentary sentences. Elsa's younger brother, Gyorg, a nimble, wiry, cheerful man in his sixties who drank nearly a bottle of vodka every night, spoke even less English than his sister. As for Gretchen and me, despite our immersion in the *Teach Yourself Norwegian* book we had been studying all summer, and my flair for languages, neither of us could communicate beyond the basics.

The so-called language barrier, as well as the so-called social and cultural barriers, were in fact no barriers for me at all. They made me gratifyingly unknowable. In New Jersey, I was transparent. Or perhaps it is more accurate to say that I felt like I was transparent. I felt that people could see right through me to the forces that had helped determine who I was. In Norway, I felt hidden and protected as if behind a window encrusted with ice and snow.

I timidly declared that I was a writer, and presto! Everyone treated me as a writer. Gretchen, who drew and painted in watercolors, was the artist. We woke up at dawn. Gretchen worked at her art and I read and wrote until dinnertime.

The part of Tromøy where Elsa lived was called Kjenna. It had its own library, which you reached by walking along a narrow path through a small forest. At least three times a week, Gretchen and I walked along that charmed path through the forest to the library. Once there we practiced reading Norwegian books, and also read the few books they had in English. Sometimes it snowed as we made our little journey, adding to the air of enchantment. One afternoon, standing at the edge of a row of shelves, reading Sylvia Plath's *The Bell Jar* in English, I noticed a Norwegian boy sitting at a table. He was about ten years younger than I was. A book lay in front of him, but he was staring out the window. For some reason, from time to time over all the years since then, the memory of him has returned to me and I have wondered what he was thinking as he looked at the world outside the window. Was it familiar? Or was it as strange to him as it was to me?

Elsa left lox on buttered bread or flatbread out for us for lunch. In the evenings, we had a simple dinner of fish or reindeer meatballs with Elsa and Gyorg. Like everything else, the reindeer meat had the dispensation of the strange. I would have eaten a fried kitten in that enchanted land of unmoored meanings. One evening, after Gretchen and I tried in tortuous

Norwegian to explain how we would never have eaten reindeer back in the States, her relatives nodded their heads appreciatively. *Erst kommt das Essen*, I said, quoting a German playwright, *dann die Moral*, which means, roughly translated, "food before morality." Gretchen blushed. The playwright was Bertolt Brecht, she told everyone. Yes, I added enthusiastically, it's from *The Threepenny Opera*, one of my favorite works of literature! Her relatives nodded respectfully. I became a figure of awesome culture. Gyorg started inviting his closest friend over to hear me speak. The two of them sat listening to me after dinner for hours, nodding in deferential miscomprehension as I, joining them in their nightly vodka binges, extemporized on the central themes of Brecht's play, and on the evolution of human knowledge in general.

A sixteenth-century French philosopher once wrote a book arguing that climate was the most important factor in the evolution of a society. I don't remember the particulars of his theory, but it is not hard to develop it from his premise. Hot climates, for example, lead to a situation where outer reality engulfs the mind and makes it languid. Outer reality grows all the more intense as the mind weakens. The heat magnifies the most trivial event. An insult becomes a blow to the ego that can only be settled by a vendetta. A woman's bareness in public threatens the stability of home. Tribal differences shatter self-esteem. Trauma inflicted by the outside world is impossible to overcome. The world must pay for it: trauma came from the outer world, and it must return to the outer world. The violation of a child's innocence results, two decades later, in the child reenacting the explosion of his innocence. He blows himself up as his young life was blasted, this time exploding other people as he was exploded.

The Scandinavian climate was just right for me. The long

nights, intense cold, and prolonged boredom of winter led to a
mental condition in which the life of the mind was more vivid
and real than the physical circumstances and events outside
the mind. Turned inward by the ice and snow, overdeveloped
imaginations exaggerated what lay beyond shuttered windows.
Mountains housed giants. Trolls populated the forests. The
sheltering mind animated every stone, tree, twig outside it as if
the physical world were actually a mass of flickering thoughts.
Maybe it was the imagination of disaster that gradually made
these societies so humane. Free health care, affordable housing,
free college tuition—they protect you against the roving mon-
sters of sickness, homelessness, crushing debt.

I began to feel that I was inhabiting a Norse fairy tale:
"The Traveler's Opacity."

A benevolent yet mischievous troll, who lived in the forest
not far from Elsa's house, became aware of my situation. Seeking to entertain his master by raising the hopes of a human to
an impossible level, he gave me the gift of being opaque. Being
a stranger in a foreign land hid my strangeness. No one could
see through me to what I feared I was. All they could see was
what I wanted them to see. I flourished so long as it lasted. I
wrote many hundreds of pages of stories and essays that tried
to make sense of what I was assimilating from all my frenzied
reading. Sometimes in the middle of the night, excited by a
thought, I would go to my desk, turn on the light, and type
in throes of ecstasy on my Smith-Corona. One night, a drunken
Gyorg opened the door to our room, having mistaken it for
his own. I liked to sleep without any clothes on. There I was,
naked, furiously typing. Gyorg smiled pleasantly, nodded to
me, and went on his way. He never brought it up, and never did
anything to make me or Gretchen think that he saw me that
night. It could be that he was so drunk that the image of me
never made it out of his stupor into his consciousness. But I
don't think so. What happened was that the troll had cast such

a magical opacity over me that even in my most naked, transparent state, I was the figure I had long nursed in my imagination: a writer fulfilling his destiny through his work.

Little by little, though, the spell began to wear off. The
troll had arranged it so that the more creative strength I drew
from my opacity, the more I drained the opacity of its power.

After two months, Gretchen and I ran out of money. We had
a few hundred dollars left over beyond our traveling expenses.
Naively assuming that at least one of us would find work in
Norway before our money ran out, we thought that our small
fund would carry us through. By the end of November, after
spending on food, small gifts now and then for Elsa and Gyorg,
and the occasional trip to a café in Arendal, the money was gone.
I could not bring myself to write to my mother to ask for her help.
When I had told her we were going to Norway to start a new life,
she laughed. Do you think you can run away from your troubles, Mr. Kafka? she said. As for Gretchen asking her mother
for money, that was impossible. Half the few hundred dollars
we had brought with us had come from her as a gift. On her
nurse's salary and her husband's income as a self-employed electrician, she had just enough money to support Gretchen's two
younger sisters and younger brother, all of whom lived at home.

I still read and wrote all day and for much of the night, but
it was becoming more difficult to gather up the will to write. The
closer we came to running out of money, the harder we tried to
find a job that would have been under the official radar. Piece by
piece, our struggles to find work chipped away at the ice and
snow that had concealed our misfittedness.

In our exuberant optimism, I had told Gretchen's family that
I was expecting money from a story I had sent out to a magazine. One day Elsa asked, with hope and cheer, if the money
was on its way, and we admitted that the story hadn't been
bought in the end. This made Elsa sad for us, but another patch
was cleared. Gradually, the heat of our desperation melted what

was left of the blessedly obscuring ice and snow. After that, I was Lee Siegel once again. It didn't matter to me that Gretchen's family had come to accept me. I felt that they had accepted me on false premises.

There was one small consolation. As we grew more transparent, our Norwegian began to improve. By the time, in mid-December, that we were all packed and ready for our trip back to New Jersey, by the time the magic spell of opacity had worn off, by the time I could barely write and began to lie awake at night worrying about how we would survive once back in New Jersey—by then, Gretchen and I were able to communicate with her family in Norwegian without any trouble at all.

# 7

# SEND MONEY, KAFKA!

Why do we experience events that change our lives in an instant as if they are happening in a dream? A car accident, the death of someone you love, the news that you have lost your job, your husband of thirty years suddenly punching you in the face one morning at breakfast—that is when reality comes crashing into our existence stronger than it ever has. Yet we feel that these catastrophic moments are dreamlike. It is our everyday reality, though, that is the true stuff of dreams. Habits; routines; assumptions that life will continue without change; presumptions that the people in our lives will not change, disappear, or die; plans for the future; expectations that our desires will be fulfilled and our ambitions realized—none of this reflects the constant flux, surprise, and disappointment that we know, in our bones, constitute the essence of what is real. But we never describe our fragile illusion of stability as being like a dream, not until our lives are almost finished. Then we say that life went by so quickly, as if in a dream! Is it only at the end of life that we see life as it really is? Or is the end of life, as it rushes upon us, one of those catastrophic experiences—the grandaddy of them all—that imparts to the rest of our life a dreamlike quality?

Of course there are those other dreams, hopes, and wishes that are not dreams at all but pillars of our reality, no matter how fantastical they are. My dream of making a life as a reader and a writer without a college degree was the stabilizing premise of my existence. Yet it led me into a stone wall of actuality that had the effect of making me feel like I was in a dream.

The night after we returned from Norway, Gretchen and I found ourselves in the kitchen of Audrey Castor. Castor had backed me up against the sink in her kitchen. She was slapping me lightly in the face, first one cheek, then the other.

I had called my mother from the airport. She was expecting us. We had nowhere else to go. Like me, Gretchen was in transition from one life to another—from the suburban girl with few opportunities to the artist struggling to find an opening in the world—and she had no friends close enough for us to prevail upon to put us up. In my case, I could not bring myself to call the few friends I had remained close to. In some symmetrical transfer of energy, the Norwegian sojourn that had used up my opacity there endowed me with a new layer of opacity back in New Jersey. Who knew what process of transformation I had undergone across the ocean? I preferred meeting new people to reuniting with the friends who could, so I feared, see right through me. As for Paul, I could not forgive him for asking us to leave his apartment before we set out for Norway. Gretchen's insistence that he was torn and doing what he had to do for the sake of his own happiness had no effect on the hostility I felt toward him.

This left my mother. In the past, she had often come through for me up to a point, after which she tipped over into madness and destruction. The trick was for me to catch her while she was performing the role of my mother, which she did from time to time if she was in revolt against Angelo, or angry at Nathan. Arriving at her house, I told myself that I had to make sure to gauge the moment when her emotional needs began to transform her from mother into rival, or adversary. Then I would make my escape.

She opened the door and greeted us with a flurry of "sweeties" and "darlings," shedding a few tears here and there. It was late in the evening. You look tired, she said. She offered us some water. I have no coffee, she said. I have to go shopping tomorrow. Then she told us the bad news: we could not stay with her. There was not enough room now that Angelo and his children had moved in. More tears. Sweetie, honey, she said to Gretchen, touching Gretchen's knee, please understand. I would give my right arm to have you here. But—she lowered her voice in a conspiratorial, accusatory whisper—Angelo brought *all three of his children*. She tossed her head in the direction of the bedrooms with contempt, as if not allowing us to stay in her house put her and us on the moral high ground. They've spread themselves all over, she said with distaste. I gazed around the kitchen and into part of the dining room. She was right about the house being in other hands. Though not a stick of furniture had changed, I could no longer recognize the house where I grew up.

I began to stand up when my mother said, Sit down, honey. I have an idea. Since her husband died some years ago, Audrey Castor has been living in a nice-size house all by herself. I'm sure she would be happy to have you stay there until you both get on your feet. Especially, my mother said, her drooping, tired face slowly lightening into a smile, after everything that I've told her about you.

The gap between rich and poor attracts so much commentary that a visitor from another planet would think the two classes were constantly at each other's throat. In fact the gap is so great that the poor never get the opportunity to clash with the rich.

The poor live too far away from them. Within classes is where you get the most violent antagonisms, the way children who are well mannered in school will come home and fight their siblings tooth and nail.

When my mother characterized Audrey Castor's house as large, she was, as usual, exaggerating someone's good fortune. It was hard for me to tell whether she did this cluelessly or with the intention of subtly putting the person in her place. Audrey Castor's house was about half the size of my mother's house. It was a saltbox with two bedrooms on a street with similar houses.

Castor herself was about fifteen years older than my mother, who was in her late forties. She had a block-shaped face. Her iron-gray hair had been cropped with almost military efficiency. Wearing loose dark pants, a windbreaker, and white tennis shoes, she was constantly bustling about the house, leaving in her small Ford, returning, then leaving again. After brusquely saying hello to Gretchen, she never looked at her again.

Alongside Castor, my mother did indeed resemble the movie-star image she harbored in that eternally childish corner of herself. My mother must have sensed, with her ultrasensitive antennae for all the degrees of self-abasement, that putting herself down was the only way to maintain the balance of their friendship. How Audrey must have drawn sustenance from my mother's tales of woe and humiliation! How my mother, having recoiled from the effects of abasing herself, then must have showered Audrey with compliments: You look stunning in that windbreaker! Cinderella should have such sneakers!

From the moment we woke up the next morning, Castor channeled her agitated energy into her encounter with me. In-sisting that we sit at her kitchen table, she served us coffee and bagels. I know how you people enjoy your bagels, she said to me. Then she began to draw me into a conversation about my future. Her conviction that she was doing the virtuous thing had clearly justified her instant intimacy with me. Behind her wise counsel was my mother's list of grievances against me, and behind her aggression was Lola's proclamation of my world-historical talents.

You need to go back to Montclair, Audrey said. Writing is not for you. Look at you. Look at what your writing has gotten you. Nothing. Not a penny to your name. Just like Monroe. Just like your father.

I was speechless for a moment. Have you ever met my father? I snapped at her.

Oh, look at this, she said. A regular sabra. A regular little Israeli soldier. No, I never met your father. Your mother told me everything I want to know about your father. About how he sold all your savings bonds from your bar mitzvah. About how he tried to take the house from your mother.

Let's go, Gretchen said to me.

I stood up to take my coffee mug over to the sink. For some reason, in my rage and confusion, I wanted to show Castor that, unlike my father, I fulfilled my obligations. She followed me across the kitchen. When I turned around after depositing the mug, she pressed me against the sink.

You are a bad boy, she said, tapping my face with her open hand. You are a bad little Jewish boy.

She was nearly as tall as I was. Beyond her I could see Gretchen rising from her chair at the kitchen table. She was trembling. I had never seen her like that. She had the shaking rage of the gentle soul who does not have a temper. Her eyes had contracted, like a cat's. Yet there was panic in them, as if her mind could not control what her body was doing. I saw her advance toward Castor and raise her mug in the air. I caught her eye and Gretchen stopped and glared at her.

*She's* not going to help you, Castor said, seeing me look at Gretchen. She doesn't need this shit from you, she said. She's a shiksa, right? She's a blond shiksa. She doesn't need this from you. She opened a drawer from under the counter and took out a steak knife. Waving it in front of my face, she said, Why are you such a bad son? Because you have a bad father?

Slowly I raised my hand and closed it around her wrist, just below the knife. I began to pull her arm down and away from my face. I didn't want to hurt her and I didn't want her to hurt Gretchen or me. I just wanted us to escape. I despised my mother for leading me into a situation where I nearly got killed in the Dodge Dart, and for putting me in this kitchen with Audrey Castor. In her frantic efforts to save herself she had gravitated toward refrigerator-sentiment people, toward anyone who gratified her need for easy attachment by means of sticky feelings. She kept sacrificing me to these people who seemed to love her so instantly and who treated her with contempt because she needed their love. Castor smiled at me as I pulled down her arm. She brought her mouth close to mine so that our lips were almost touching. She stared at me and I stared back. After a minute or so, the situation became too absurd to continue. She stepped away from me.

Go back to school, she said with a show of stern affection, as if she had contrived the entire incident for the purpose of representing my mother's interests and making me more serious about life; as if that was the only decent thing for her to do. Don't break your mother's heart, she said.

I took Gretchen's arm. The two of us walked back to the small bedroom. We locked the door and sat holding each other on the bed. After we heard Audrey leave, I went to the phone near the front door and called Angelo at his school. Though he sounded wary, and put out at being disturbed at work, he listened solemnly as I told him what had happened. Sit tight, he said. An hour later, he picked us up and drove us in silence away from Castor's house.

I believed that so long as I did not make myself yet another plague on his vulnerable nerves, Angelo would do what he

could to help me. In this case, all he had to do was convince my
mother to allow us to stay in the den or the basement for a
week or so, until I could find another job or jobs in the malls.
I turned to Gretchen, who was sitting in the backseat. She
placed her hand on my shoulder for a moment before withdraw-
ing it. After a few minutes, Angelo turned onto the highway.
Then he pulled off into the parking lot of a motel. It was the
one cheap motel in Paramus, right across the highway from
Alexander's.

I can give you enough money to stay for a week, Angelo
said. He got out of the car, removed our bags from the trunk,
and set them down on the parking lot. Cars were racing by on
the highway. I wondered if anyone I knew or had been to high
school with saw me. After that, Angelo said, I can't help you.
He took some bills out of his wallet, handed them to me without looking at me, and sat back in the car. Good luck, he said
to me, extending his hand, which I mechanically shook. And if
I were you, he said, smiling at me with that gentle air of complicity, I wouldn't tell your mother about what happened with
Audrey. Then he drove off.


The motel was forty dollars a night. Angelo, in his rush to help
us out as quickly as possible, had only given me a hundred and
twenty. Thanks to Gretchen's mother, who brought us eighty
dollars after we called her as a last resort, we were able to stay
for five days. She also lent us her car, an old station wagon with
a manual shift on the steering column that only Gretchen knew
how to drive. We would not have lasted in the motel much beyond a week anyway. The sheets had large stains on them and
were stiff in places. Pubic hair was all over them. We stripped
the sheets off the bed, turned the discolored mattress over, and
slept on that. I thought of calling Einman, but I did not want
him to see me in such a despondent state. We might have to go

live in the park, I said to Gretchen in an anxious joke one night as we lay on the mattress on the floor, trying to sleep amid the constant whoosh of cars on the highway.

Not wanting to spend any more time in the motel room than we had to, we left in the morning as soon as it became light. We drove to a donut place where we sat drinking coffee until the malls opened and I could make the rounds once again, looking for work. Within a few days, thanks to my experience at Herman's, I found a job selling shoes at a small store called Fit to Be Tied, located in one of the Paramus malls. Gretchen landed a part-time job as a waitress at a Howard Johnson's on Route 4, not far from our motel.

Fortified by seemingly stable jobs, we went looking for an apartment. Gretchen's mother promised to help us out with the deposit and the first month's rent. She probably had to dip into some sort of savings account that she had set up apart from her joint finances with her husband. She continued to regard me with wary puzzlement, as if prepared for any sudden gesture I might make that could put her daughter's life in mortal danger. But since Gretchen had thrown her lot in with mine so wholeheartedly, her mother had decided that the most effective way to keep Gretchen safe was to try as well as she could to protect both of us. I sometimes felt, to my embarrassment, that I was a cobeneficiary along with Gretchen's father of her wise tolerance. Fairly quickly we were able to find a tiny studio in a three-story apartment building in Bergenfield, about fifteen minutes from Paramus.

Fit to Be Tied was a women's shoe store. I worked full-time, five days a week. Sometimes I had the early shift, and sometimes the evening shift, which began in the late afternoon and ended at nine at night. Still resolved, though shaken, to make a life for myself as a reader and a writer without returning to college,

I had told Tim, the store manager, that I wished to build a career at the store. So long as I remained committed to the job, Tim and the other salesmen there—the reasoning went that women were more likely to be flattered by a man into purchasing shoes than by a woman, and this proved to be correct—found my frequent allusions to culture endearing and entertaining. I made them in order to remind myself of who I was and who I aspired to be. Whenever my pride reared up, and I gave the impression that I had aspirations beyond ambitions at the store, they began to regard me with defensive disdain. To protect myself, I fell back into the old role of clown. Standing in the back of the store, in the doorway of the stockroom, I would proceed to imagine what various customers were thinking as they tried on shoes. I did this in different accents, depending on the particular customer's ethnic background.

The erotic atmosphere of buying and selling things that I had felt working in Alexander's was a full-blown reality at Fit to Be Tied. Tim's deputy, Anthony, an Italian American with a muscular pot belly and perpetual stubble, and Patrick, Anthony's slight, handsome Irish American pal, sometimes had sex with various customers in the stockroom in exchange for shoes. Women love shoes, Anthony said to me with a self-satisfied smile. With the exception of Tim, who was the store's royalty and thus bound to his position as austere overseer, having sex with customers was part of the culture of the place. You should try it, Anthony said. I don't think anyone is very interested in me, I said. We'll fix you up, he said. I told him I was shy. Shy? he repeated. The expression on his face was about to tip over into that derisive disdain. You know, I said, Gretchen keeps me busy. Anthony and the others remained suspicious. I related all this to Gretchen, who shook her head in contempt. One warm spring afternoon she surprised me by coming into the store dressed in a halter top, denim shorts, and clogs. After that, instead of goading me into the store's debauched atmosphere—they felt some high-minded

disapproval in my demurral and could not tolerate it—Anthony
and Patrick apparently decided to impose a limit on my success
with women and kept me away from the more fetching customers. This was for my own good, they told me. Still, the sexual
atmosphere was so present and so intense that I sometimes disappeared into the men's room to masturbate when an attractive
woman came in for shoes. Getting lost in some imaginary future
encounter as if it was happening in that very moment, I finished
quickly, with excitement. Afterward I felt drained and exhausted.
It was a while before I could look people in the eye while talking
with them.

My single friend at Fit to Be Tied was the one black salesman there. You are my *sole* friend here, I intoned. He groaned. His
name was Luke. He had been a high school basketball star, but
an injured leg prevented him from getting a scholarship to college. Needing to work full-time, unable to pay for college even
as a part-time student, he took a job at the store, where he had
worked for several years. Luke and I were assigned the task of
keeping the narrow stockroom's shelves full. Together we carried large boxes out from the loading dock into the stockroom,
and then shelved and reshelved the individual boxes of shoes
that were in them. We often spent our lunch hours together,
eating hamburgers and fries at a small metal table alongside
the mall's fountain. Coins shimmered beneath the undulating
water.

Luke told me about his glory days and about the afternoon
he tore up his leg, knowing with certainty, the instant he hit
the ground writhing in pain, that his future was lost to him. I
spoke of Bradley, and Bergner's, the gas station and Montclair
and Norway, and about my aspirations to become a writer. When
I told him the story about the shoplifter in Bergner's, he laughed.
That was probably my cousin, he said. He was white, I said.
Luke considered me thoughtfully.

One day, as we sat sipping our Cokes through straws, watching the jet of water shooting into the air and falling in thick plumes of droplets back into the pool below, Luke said, What are you doing here, man?

What are *you* doing here? I said. I thought he meant that I was unfit to sell shoes. I began to worry about my job.

Where am I going to go? he said. I'm lucky to be here at all. I have some fine women in my life, though.

Luke didn't leer when he talked about sex, like the other salesmen in the store. He talked about it with a kind of reverence. He refused to have sex with customers in exchange for shoes, a choice that went unquestioned by Anthony and Patrick on account of Luke's clear authority as a physical presence. He still possessed an athlete's beauty and grace, though he squandered his vitality in New York sex clubs, to which he would go just about every weekend with one woman or another. Yet in some strange way, he was fulfilling his destiny in a tributary off the dammed-up river of his physical gifts. A large hole had been blasted in his self-esteem. Gratifying women and being gratified by them revived his inborn balance of mind and body. It did not offend me that he sometimes referred to women as bitches. I thought of my mother as a bitch. He, on the other hand, worshipped his mother and his grandmother. But so much of his life had been put beyond the controlling reach of his talents that he needed, in the way he used language, to control whatever his talents were able to attain. Then, too, since women had become the exclusive source of his strength, he had to establish a counterweight to their dominance. So these figures of nourishment and grace, whom he sought to win and to please, became bitches he enjoyed the illusion of mastering.

But he loved women. When Gretchen came into the store wearing her provocative outfit, Anthony and Patrick looked her over with a brazenness that bordered on insult. Luke, however, having heard me describe Gretchen's aspirations, immediately drew her into a conversation about her art. He never let his eyes wander from hers, yet he never tried to hold her gaze, either. He was one of those people, like Ned, blessed with bountiful understanding and intuition, gifts that society offered no remunerative place for unless they were accompanied by a drive for self-advancement, which was a whole different quality altogether. We became close without becoming real friends. Once or twice, when I emerged from the bathroom drenched in shame from my exertions, Luke gently put his arm on mine for a second. Our different escapes into empty pleasures brought both of us pain.

Like many sexual beings, Luke's extensive experience of the secret entanglements of thought, feeling, pleasure, and power gave him an intimate conversance with life's subtleties. He was easy for me to talk to.

One day Luke said, I'm applying for a job as a mailman. Anthony and these guys, they're nowhere, man. Nowhere. I got to get out of here.

I see what you mean, I said.

You want me to get you an application, too? he said.

Immediately my head filled with thoughts of life as a mailman, wearing a uniform, earning a steady income, driving a cool truck.

Yes, I said. I'd like that.

You've got to get out of here, too, man. You've just got to.

I nodded. But when, a few days later, he brought in the application for me, I thanked him and stuck it between some books on a shelf when I got home. I might have been struggling on the margins like Luke, but I did not feel that I had to settle for a job that did not fulfill me. In this case, social destiny had spotted me precious yards. He was black, and I was white.

•

Without Gretchen I was lost. With her, I was beginning to feel overburdened. She loved me so completely that she left it to me to decide which direction we should go in. I mistook her love for me for a passive inability to assert her own wants—despite the fact that if she had had the conventional desire for prosperity and family, I would not have been able to fulfill it. I could not see how aligned with me she was. I had become so emotionally corrupted by my dependence on her that I was unable to recognize the integrity of her attachment to me. Instead I felt that I had to provide twice the horsepower to launch us forward, out of our circumstances into the future. I was blind to the fact that she had decided that I was her future, and that she would accept any present we found ourselves in together. It bothered me also that she accepted our reduced circumstances—circumstances that I had led us into—without complaint.

When we moved into the Bergenfield studio, we had been unable to afford mattresses and slept on the floor in sleeping bags. Even after we had the money to buy an inexpensive full-size mattress, we remained in the sleeping bags. Gretchen was trying, without success, to draw in watercolors. She had taken a second part-time job in a telemarketing office not far from our apartment, and whenever she had time to herself was too tired to work. I had dragged a discarded kitchen table off the curb in front of someone's house into the station wagon. Setting it up in the apartment, I put the Smith-Corona on it and sat down to write. But nothing came. My opacity was all used up. I could not get any traction going. I felt that I had no life to start from. I had given the post office my new address and was having my old mail forwarded from my mother's house. One day a letter arrived, demanding that I start paying several hundred dollars a month on the loans I had taken out to attend Bradley and Montclair. I threw it into the garbage in disgust and disbelief.

At Montclair, I craved a more enlightened, cosmopolitan

atmosphere. I felt liberated when I left. But my isolated poles of existence, at Fit to Be Tied and in our apartment, were growing unendurable. We had bought some cheap metal shelving and I had lined the walls of the apartment with books. But instead of being the magic portals they had always been, the rows of books became barriers between me and the world outside the studio's single window.

One day, after putting down a book by Herman Melville that I had been reading, I noticed on the back of it the address of the book's publisher, the New American Library. The New American Library was an august publisher of classic works of literature, mostly American, and it was right there, in Bergenfield! I had read so many books that appeared under its imprint that the mere sight of one of their volumes made me feel like I was in the presence of family—my true family. Perhaps I could find work there as an editor. I imagined sitting at a desk piled high with manuscripts, surrounded by literary people, receiving a steady income for the joy of reading.

In the morning on one of my days off, I set out for their offices. I knew that if I followed the railroad tracks that ran behind our building, I could find them. The walk was longer than I thought. After what seemed like an hour, I scrambled down the embankment from the tracks and turned onto a dead-end street lined with low, windowless rectangular buildings. I had brought the Melville with me to confirm the address. There it was. What I had imagined was the New American Library's editorial offices was its warehouse.

A few days later, I roused myself from dejection. To my sudden delight, I remembered that I had left the two boxes of stories and essays with Angelo before leaving for Norway. I drove up to my mother's house one Sunday to reclaim them. Fit to Be Tied was closed and Gretchen was at Howard Johnson's. I figured that going back to some of my older work would give me the boost I needed to start writing again. I was also relieved at the thought of having something to read that I had written instead of staring at a blank page.

It was the middle of the day. Angelo came to the door. My mother, he said, was asleep. I reminded him of the boxes and told him that I had come to pick them up. Boxes? he said. What boxes? The boxes of stories and essays that I left with you before going to Norway, I said. Oh, he said, with an amiable smile, I had to throw them out. We just didn't have the room. He made his declaration casually, in good humor, as if it was understood that we both shared the same aversion to trouble and clutter. Hadn't the secret agreement between us to avoid trouble with my mother been responsible for him agreeing to hold on to the boxes to begin with? The situation had changed, but the objective was the same. No trouble. No problem. There was not a hint of underlying aggression or hostility to me in his attitude. There was simply his belief that I did not deserve anything more out of this life than he did. And that this was a natural cause of solidarity between us.


Ever since I was a boy, standing on the overpass that crossed Route 17 and looking at the Empire State Building in a quivering blue haze that was either how it appeared or the product of my emotions, I had been under the spell of Manhattan. In high school my friends and I had made breathless trips to the city, where we waited outside jazz clubs we could not afford to get into to talk to the musicians who emerged through the stage door when the night was over. I thought of New York as a teeming maelstrom that inverted or reversed the markers people used to sum you up. For all my desire to remake myself, I had always been afraid that I would lose myself in that commotion. Now, exhausted by my own shortcomings and by the limitations of where I found myself, I had nothing to lose. Gretchen, an aspiring artist who made almost weekly pilgrimages to the city's museums and art galleries, with me in tow, was thrilled by the idea of living in New York.

At the same time, from the moment I stood on the campus of the University of Chicago, surrounded by those thick limestone walls, I knew that I belonged at a university. I thought that there my weaknesses and my strengths could be protected. The more enlightened and stimulating the university, the more, I believed, my weaknesses would be tolerated, even addressed in some way, and my strengths developed.

I began to spend all my off-hours in the Bergenfield library, poring over the college catalogs of public universities in New York that the university had on microfilm. Finally I narrowed them down to two: Brooklyn College and Queens College. My criterion for choosing them was my excited discovery of various distinguished writers, poets, and scholars who taught at one or the other of them.

On one of my days off during the week, when Gretchen was working at the telemarketer, I took several buses to the Brooklyn College campus in the heart of Brooklyn. A young Russian woman who worked in the admissions office, where I asked questions about requirements and about financial aid that had not been covered in the catalogs, smiled at me. She had lustrous dark eyes and I could not get her out of my mind for days afterward. To keep the thought of her at bay, I kept asking Gretchen to imagine with me what our life might be like in New York.


A short time after my trip to Brooklyn, Gretchen and I were lying on our sleeping bags, reading the Sunday *New York Times*. Look at this, she said. It was a full-page ad for an undergraduate program at something called the School of General Studies at Columbia University. According to the ad, the program was designed for older students who had, "for one reason or another," not finished their bachelor's degree. Students from diverse backgrounds were encouraged to apply. One phrase stood out for me: "Academic scholarships are available."

Behind my resolve to make a life for myself without a college degree had been the certainty of rejection from the kind of school I longed to be at. The cost of a school like Columbia embodied my sense of exclusion. Even with a loan, I had barely been able to afford Montclair without working part-time. Tuition at a place like Columbia, far more than it had been at Bradley, was the equivalent of a barbed-wire fence.

That Sunday I began to have a different perspective. For one thing, the ad for Columbia rested in the hands of someone who had faith in me. For another, my desperation led me to take chances I never would have considered when my hopefulness that everything would turn out okay made me cautious. Most decisive of all was the fact that, academically, I was in a different place. I had not done well enough in high school to qualify for an academic scholarship at Bradley, and I had not done well enough at Bradley to win an academic scholarship there or at Montclair. But I believed that my grades at Montclair were sufficient to get me financial aid based on merit at Columbia.

The next day I called Columbia to request an application and rounded up the necessary transcripts and recommendations. I labored for days on a several-thousand-word personal essay that was a required part of the admissions process. A few weeks after I applied, I received an acceptance letter in the mail. I was so astonished that I called the admissions office to make sure that there had not been some sort of mistake.

I had sent a note to Einman to see if he would be willing to write me a recommendation. He immediately sat down and wrote what I assume, because of the surprising result, was a glowing letter. But though I wrote to thank him, I ignored the several notes he sent in reply asking to see me, and I was never in touch with him again. My flight from my father had become a universal

reaction to anyone from my past who reminded me of me. Einman was a citizen of my past, governed by the bizarre rules I
had devised in my attempt to escape from that narrow country.

Admission to Columbia had its obstacles, which I had expected. Though I had attended Bradley for two years and Montclair for one, Columbia would only accept credits that added up
to one year of academic work. That meant that I would need
three more years of full-time attendance to get my BA, at which
point I would be twenty-six. But this was yet another impedi-
ment that, for me, presented itself as an opportunity. The longer
I could find refuge within the protective walls of a university, and
a great, cosmopolitan university at that, the better it was.

The more daunting obstacle was money. I was right about
my performance at Montclair winning me a modest scholarship
at Columbia. But after the Pell Grant and other forms of aid, I
still owed a hefty amount of tuition, though the financial aid
people at Columbia assured me that if I did well during my first
year, I could receive enough scholarship money to pay my way
after that.

Once again, I applied for a loan. This time I was turned
down. I had defaulted on my earlier loans and I was not eligible
for any new ones until I paid them off. Repaying the loans
outright, however, was beyond the realm of possibility. The
interest rate was 9 percent and by now the amount I owed had
ballooned to nearly seven thousand dollars. And as I learned
during the course of several frantic phone calls to the New Jersey
Department of Higher Education, the agency that was admin-
istering the loans, it was too late to set up a monthly payment
schedule, even if I could have afforded it.

I refused to give up. Feeling that my back was against the
wall was the situation I felt most comfortable in. I called again
and again, dismissing the final judgment of everyone I spoke
to. I turned a lack of dignity and pride into an almost unstoppa-

ble force, submerging my ego in a desperate energy. I drew my energy from disappointment and self-abasement. These were the springs of despair for most people, but for me they were a return to the sources of all my efforts to remake myself. After a while, I thought I could tell from the sound of an agent's voice how responsive he or she was. I started hanging up if I did not find someone's tone promising. Then one day, after countless calls, a woman named Mrs. Zagnit answered the phone.

I must have started off with an incoherent rush of words in an attempt to describe my situation, because the first thing she did was tell me to calm down. Shhh, she said, as if to a child. Shhh. Then she asked me to slowly and briefly give an account of my situation. After I managed to do so, she patiently laid out for me what my obligations had been when I signed for the loan, and why I had to fulfill them before taking out another. I listened to her without interrupting. After she finished, I told her the story of how Gretchen and I had reached the point we were at. I worked backward in time, telling her about Norway, and living in my mother's house, and Bradley, and my parents' divorce, and my father's bankruptcy. I wanted her to feel sorry for me. Pity can be the midwife of mercy, and mercy, I was convinced, was the only emotion strong enough to curb the law. Yet I spoke plainly and tersely. I felt that any hint of manipulative emotion or self-pity would strain her patience. She seemed to be listening, as if to a heartbeat, to something underneath my circumstances. She wanted to know who this person was beneath the statistical problem. Finally I declared that there was an absurd distance between the precious intangibles of my life and my material circumstances. I said it just like that: it was a line from one of my stories. She laughed, not mockingly but in surprise. She was silent for a moment, and then she said:

I will make one exception for you, but only this once. If you don't meet your obligations after this, you will not get a second chance. If you can send me five hundred dollars, I will authorize you to take out another loan. Do you have five hundred dollars?

Yes, I said. Absolutely.

Are you sure? she said.

Yes, I said. I can get it to you.

And will you repay this loan? she asked me.

Yes, I will, I said. Dear God, I meant it. I meant it with all my heart.

She was silent again. It was nice to talk with you, she said, after transforming my life, with one gesture, by breaking the cardinal rule that she had been assigned to enforce. Good luck, she said.


My mother was the last person I wanted to ask for the money, and she was the only person I could ask for the money. I sped toward the inevitable encounter up the Garden State Parkway at about eighty miles per hour. Parking in front of the old split-level, I jumped out of the car and bounded up the steps onto the front stoop. The faster I could do this, the faster it would be over.

Lola came to the door in her nightgown. It was about three in the afternoon. Yes, honey, she said wearily. I explained the situation to her. I was breathing heavily. We stood there staring at each other, two different people in a force field of genetic complicity, absolutely opposed to each other. She laughed. Why don't you ask your father? she said. You know he has no money, I said. But I have no money! she cried. Here we go, I said. Here we go. That's right, she hissed. Here we go. Here we go because you dream and dream and dream, like your father, and like your father, everyone else has to pay for your dreams. Do you think I owe you this money? Do you? No, I said. I don't think you owe me anything. I'm asking you to loan it to me, that's all. I'll pay it back. Like you paid back your loans? she said. I'll pay it back, I said. Enough, she said. Enough. I brought you into the world. Do you know how much that hurt? It hurt a lot. Try it sometime. It's not easy to bring another person into the world. Then I cleaned you. I wiped you. I soothed you when you cried. I stayed up all night with you. Do you know how tired I am? Do you know how many nights I stayed up with you and how tired I am? This is my one chance to have a better life, I said. To be where I belong. Please lend me the money. Mr. Kafka, she said. Mr. Kafka doesn't like where he is. He always wants to be somewhere else. Montclair was not good enough for you. You had a career ahead of you in the shoe store. Audrey Castor could have helped you, but no, you had to go and push her away. Yes, I know all about that. Thank you very much. Audrey knows people at the Board of Education. Thank you very much. Do you think a fancy school is going to change you, Mr. Kafka? Huh? Do you think your books are going to save you? Huh, Mr. Kafka? Mr. Tolstoy? Mr. Prowst? Proost, I said. It's pronounced Proost. Oh, my little professor. Well, Proost thanked his mother for wiping him, believe me. Kafka didn't keep his mother up all night while he talked with his girlfriends on the phone. Get the money from Kafka. Ask Kafka. Kafka! she yelled into the front yard. Send money! Send money, Kafka! You're nuts, I said. You are out of your fucking mind. I turned around. Goodbye, I said. I'll find the money somehow. I walked down the stairs into the front yard. Fuck it, I thought. People like you don't go to Columbia. You have Gretchen. You have the shoe store. Luke will get you into the post office. This is the way it was meant to be. All this suffering will lead to something. People go through worse in life. *Je m'en fous.* Wait a minute! my mother cried. She disappeared. Then she appeared again. Holding something between the fingers of her right hand, she raised her hand in the air. Take my engagement ring, she said. It's the only expensive piece of jewelry I have. Take it and sell it. Here, she said. She threw it into the yard. Take it. Take the only precious thing I have. Go ahead. That's what a mother does for her son, she said. I dropped to my knees and crawled around in the grass for a few minutes before I felt the ring under my hand. Did you find it? she asked. Yes, I said. Getting to my feet, I climbed back up the steps to where she stood in the doorway. Now you're too proud? she said, her eyes glinting with satisfaction. No, I said. I took her hand and pressed the ring into it. You sell it, I said. Then send me the money. Her face began to twitch. She started to cry. You son of a bitch, she said. You coldhearted son of a bitch.

Three days later a check from her for five hundred dollars arrived in the mail.

In late August of that year, I was on a subway traveling uptown under Broadway. If I had stayed on the train to the end of the line, I would have passed the stop at 231st Street, just a block from where I had once said goodbye to Menka. Columbia, though, was at 116th Street. When I emerged from underground, the sun was blazing overhead. I crossed the street. Then I strode through the university's wide-open wrought-iron gates, toward the bursar and my new life.

# Acknowledgments

My committed and unsparing editor, Ileene Smith, has wisdom and heart. My exquisitely astute agent, Markus Hoffmann, has stood by me through thick and thin.

Three dear, gifted friends read the manuscript. Their enlightening responses helped bring the book to completion.

Without my wife, Christina Gillham, and our children, Julian and Harper, I would not have been able to tell this tale at all.

# A NOTE ABOUT THE AUTHOR

Lee Siegel is the author of five previous books and the recipient of a National Magazine Award. A widely published writer on culture and politics, he lives with his family in Montclair, New Jersey.